I0532410

BOSS

Business Owner's Secret Sauce

THE RECIPE FOR SUCCESS

Natalia Alaine

Copyright © 2023 by Natalia Alaine

All rights reserved.

No portion of this book may be reproduced in any form without written permission from the publisher or author, except as permitted by U.S. copyright law.

The advice and strategies contained herein may not be suitable for your situation. You should consult with a professional when appropriate. Neither the publisher nor the author shall be liable for any loss of profit or any other commercial damages, including but not limited to special, incidental, consequential, personal, or other damages.

This publication is designed to provide accurate and authoritative Information in regard to the subject matter covered. The reader acknowledges that the author does not provide any specific tax advice, legal advice, or investment advice and that for any of these matters the reader will consult with licensed professionals.

All brand names and product names used in this book are trademarks, registered trademarks, or trade names of their respective holders. The author is not associated with any product or vendor in this book.

We would like to bring to your attention that any internet addresses, company or product information printed in this book are provided solely as a resource and are not intended to be, or to imply an endorsement of the content or services of these sites, beyond this book. It is imperative that you exercise due diligence when working with any of the companies referenced in this book.

This book is written as a source of information only. The information contained in this book should by no means be considered a substitute for the advice, decisions, or judgment of the reader's professional or financial advisors. All efforts have been made to ensure the accuracy of the information contained in this book as of the date published. The author and the publisher expressly disclaim responsibility for any adverse effects arising from the use or application of the information contained

Paperback ISBN: 979-8-9880285-1-2
HC ISBN: 979-8-9880285-0-5
eBook ISBN: 979-8-9880285-2-9

Emma and Sol, this book is dedicated to you both. You are my North Star, lighting up my world and giving me the motivation to keep pushing forward. I can't wait to see all the incredible things you'll achieve.

"The moment you doubt whether you can fly, you cease forever to be able to do it."

– PETER PAN

CONTENTS

INTRODUCTION

Starting something new is always thrilling. Whether it's the chance of success or the possibility of improvement, it brings a rush of excitement that's hard to describe. While I'm not an author, I'm a serial entrepreneur who has bought, sold, owned, created, invested, and occasionally failed at different businesses. I don't have any strict guidelines on what type of businesses I'm willing to get into. Trash companies, appliance rentals, marketing firms, pack and ship stores, real estate - I love them all the same.

But my enthusiasm for starting something new isn't just limited to my own ventures - it's contagious! When I see others taking the plunge, I become a cheerleader on steroids, ready to help them plan and succeed. I can't help it - being an entrepreneur is just part of my DNA. It's who I am, through and through.

There's something about entrepreneurship that speaks to me on a fundamental level. It's not just about making money or being your own boss - it's about creating something from nothing, and watching it grow and thrive. Whether it's a tech startup or a mom-and-pop store, the idea of building something meaningful and impactful is what drives me.

Over the last 20 years, I've learned that being an entrepreneur isn't just a job - it's a way of life. It requires grit, determination, and a willingness to take risks. But the rewards are worth it - the sense of accomplishment, the freedom to chart your own course, and the satisfaction of knowing you've made a difference. That's what keeps me going, and that's why I'm always ready to cheer on others who share the same passion for entrepreneurship.

I've found that the challenges and questions tend to be universal, no matter the industry or type of business. It's like trying to solve a Rubik's cube - the colors may be different, but the solutions tend to be the same.

This book serves as your guide to the ups and downs of starting and running a business, providing you with the tools and insights needed to succeed no matter what comes your way. From mastering bookkeeping and executing an effective marketing strategy, to understanding your target audience and managing the often unpredictable people aspect, this book has you covered.

If you come across a chapter that doesn't seem relevant, It's all good - just skip ahead to the next one. The last thing I want is for you to waste time on material that won't help you achieve your goals.

That being said, I encourage you to read every chapter if you can. You never know what nuggets of wisdom or inspiration might be waiting for you. My hope is that this book will be a valuable resource for you, and that you'll come away with the tools and knowledge you need to succeed.

Chapter 1

PASSION IS NOT THE KEY

Someone once asked me what the least important thing in business was, and let me tell you, that got me thinking! As a lover of all things creative and cool, I've always been a big believer in turning your passion into a successful business. But the truth is, passion alone isn't always enough to make it work. Those catchy slogans like "do what you love, and you'll never work a day in your life" and "the money will follow" may sound great, but they can be seriously misleading.

The reality is that in the business world, you need a solid plan, a good strategy, and some financial savvy to make it all work. But don't panic, I'm not saying you should give up on your passions and settle for a boring desk job. Oh no, no, no! What I am saying is that you need to be strategic and smart about how you approach things.

Whenever I hear phrases like "turn your passion into profit," I can't help but think that what people really mean is to use your expertise and knowledge to create a successful business. But, if your passion isn't generating the big bucks, then start a different business that does and use the profits to support your passion. When you're starting out, don't limit yourself to just your passions. Instead, do your research, scope out the market, and identify opportunities with potential for serious income. Once you've got a good foundation, you can use that success to fuel your passions.

Remember, just because you love doing something doesn't mean you'll love doing it as a business. Once your passion becomes your primary source of income, it can quickly become a tedious chore. So if you want to turn your passion into a successful business, make sure you keep market research, skillset, and profitability top of mind. Trust me, it's the key to building a thriving business that you love.

If you look at some of the most successful businesses out there, you'll find that most owners may not be passionate about the products they sell. For example, the CEO of a successful vacuum cleaner company may not necessarily love vacuuming.

I used to own a trash company, and I can promise you I'm not exactly passionate about garbage! These days, I own a washer and dryer rental company, and while I'm not a huge fan of doing laundry, I do love the passive income it provides. What's even better is that this business is fueling my passions and providing me with the income I need to live the lifestyle I want. Sure, I may not be in love with washers and dryers, but I am in love with the freedom and opportunities that come with a successful business. Let the income generated by your business support the things you're truly passionate about.

Of course, there are exceptions to this. If you have a strong personal conviction or a cause that you deeply believe in, then you can certainly turn that into a successful business. But for most of us, the key is to find joy and fulfillment in the process. For instance, if you love being around people, you may get a kick out of interacting with customers and employees. On the other hand, if you're a number-cruncher at heart, you might enjoy diving into analytics and finding trends and insights.

The idea of doing something for "money" can be a sensitive subject, and discussing it can make people feel uncomfortable. But let's face it, money plays a crucial role in our lives and can be a powerful tool for pursuing our dreams and helping others. Money is not the root of all evil; it's actually a super useful tool for achieving our aspirations. Whether we want to indulge in a fun hobby or support a charitable cause, having financial resources is key to making it happen.

Don't get me wrong, money isn't everything. However, being passionate but broke won't benefit you, your business, or anyone else. It's important for you to find a balance between profitability and passion. So, let your imagination run wild and dream big. With the right mindset and a commitment to success, you can create a well-rounded and successful business that benefits you and the people around you. Let's make money magic happen!

Chapter 2

BET ON YOURSELF

Regular people become successful business owners all the time. Most don't have a high IQ, a rare skill set or a college degree - all it takes is a willingness to bet on yourself. Who knows, you might just be the next big thing!

Entrepreneurship is a proven path to wealth, with 88% of millionaires being entrepreneurs and 68% of them self-made. In 2022, there were over 33 million businesses, with entrepreneurs making up a significant portion of the adult workforce at 16%. The key to success in business is not rocket science. With effort and the right resources, anyone can turn their entrepreneurial dreams into a reality.

Starting a business is all about embracing the unknown and having the courage to take a leap of faith. With the right combination of determination, drive, and a solid plan, you can make your entrepreneurial dreams a reality. But beware, it also requires letting go of that cozy comfort zone and diving headfirst into uncharted territory. The reward of turning your dream into a thriving reality is priceless, so don't let fear or the false sense of security hold you back.

Many people mistakenly choose the "security" of a traditional 8-to-5 job over entrepreneurship, but this sense of security is often just an illusion. The reality is that in the face of downsizing, the boss is always the last one standing. Take the reins of your stability and become your own boss. Becoming an entrepreneur is actually the easiest job to secure, as you hold the power to make the ultimate hiring decision - that is, hiring yourself.

Just start taking baby steps, one foot in front of the other. And when the road gets rough (because let's face it, it's going to be a bumpy ride), hold on tight to your inner stubbornness and keep charging forward like a boss. The power to turn your entrepreneurial dreams into a reality is in your hands.

It may sound cliché, but the truth often is. The advice you've heard before about taking control of your life and pursuing your dreams is backed by the experiences of countless successful business owners. Don't dismiss the tried and true - take hold of it and make it your own. Go all in and bet on your own abilities, as you have the potential to achieve great things.

Chapter 3

MASTERING THE MARKET

An idea is not the same as an opportunity. I'm going to repeat that one more time, so let it sink in. AN IDEA IS NOT THE SAME AS AN OPPORTUNITY! Sure, your idea might sound fantastic, but that doesn't necessarily mean it's a viable business opportunity. To succeed, you need to do your homework and validate your idea through some serious market research. This means identifying the needs and desires of your potential customers and figuring out whether your idea can hold its own in the market.

To assess the potential of your idea as a business opportunity, you need to ask yourself two key questions and find the answers:

1) Is there enough demand for your product or service.
2) What are the unmet needs in the market that your business can fill.

By answering these two key questions, you can significantly boost your chances of success! Knowing the level of demand for your idea enables you to customize it to meet the needs of your customers. And when you identify unaddressed needs in the market, you can create a value proposition that's distinctive and sets you apart from your competitors!

Ready to take the market by storm? With the power of the internet, conducting market research is a piece of cake. Say hello to your new best friend: Google. It's your go-to source for finding information about your potential product or service and the competition.

Think of it like a treasure hunt. The answers to these questions are the clues that will lead you to the treasure trove of success. And the more thoroughly you research and validate your ideas, the closer you get to striking gold. So, don't skip out on the research phase! It's the foundation of a successful business.

To research demand for your business idea, there is a helpful tool that you can use: Google Trends. This website allows you to see how many people are searching for your product or service, which can give you an idea of the level of demand. To get started, simply go to https://trends.google.com, type in your search term, and hit enter. If you want to target a specific area, make sure to include your location in the search, and try different variations of your keyword to obtain a more accurate picture. Google Trends lets you search by day, month, or year, so you can track changes in demand over time. Don't forget to take notes of your findings, so you can refer to them later. Armed with this information, you can make informed decisions about the feasibility of your business idea and adjust your approach accordingly.

But what if you don't see many searches for your idea? That's when you'll need to focus on social media and educating people about what you're selling or inventing. It's not impossible, but it will require some effort and a hefty marketing budget.

Now, seeing a high volume of searches doesn't necessarily mean you've struck gold. You'll also need to assess the competition and find a way to stand out in the market. Next, head to Google and type in your keyword to see how many competitors you're up against. What makes your product or service unique? How does it stand out from the rest? For example, if you're selling something as common as underwear, you'll need a creative strategy to compete with the thousands of other sellers in the market. So, don't just stop at Google Trends – make sure you have a solid plan to stand out and succeed!

Go on a digital tour of your industry and examine the websites of your competitors. Assess their branding, website aesthetics, and customer reviews. The purpose is to spot opportunities for differentiating yourself and securing a share of the market. Becoming a successful entrepreneur means finding your niche and solving a problem.

For E-Commerce: When exploring potential sales channels for your product or service, consider alternative platforms. Some examples are e-commerce websites like Etsy or Amazon. By researching these marketplaces and determining if they are a good fit for your product, you can increase your reach and tap into a wider customer base. Evaluate the potential benefits and drawbacks of selling through these channels, such as fees, competition, and the target audience, to make an informed decision on the best platform for your business.

If you are planning to sell your products on Amazon, there are several useful tools that can help you estimate the sales volume for a specific product. Tools like Scope and Jungle Scout's Sales Estimator can provide valuable insights into the sales performance of your product. In addition, Amazon maintains a list of its best-selling items on its website (www.amazon.com/Best-Sellers), which can give you an idea of the products that are currently in high demand on the platform. By utilizing these tools and resources, you can make informed decisions about your product's demand and develop effective strategies to maximize your sales potential.

In this stage of your research, you'll want to pay close attention to your competitors' pricing strategies, shipping, and delivery options. While it's important to know what you're up against in terms of pricing, you'll also want to take a look at how they handle the delivery process. Do they offer free delivery to sweeten the deal for potential customers? Or do they provide express shipping options for those who simply can't wait to get their hands on your amazing product? These are all important factors to consider, and they can play a major role in the purchasing decisions of your customers.

For the service industry: In the local services industry, it's important to differentiate yourself from the competition. To do this, gather information by calling your top competitors and take note of their wait time, phone answer times, and team size. This will give you a good understanding of demand and help guide your business strategy. Ultimately, understanding your competition is key to providing exceptional service and standing out in the market.

Find out what your competitors are doing right and where they may be falling short. This information can help guide you in developing a pricing strategy and delivery process that will give you an edge in the market and help you stand out. The key to success is finding your unique place in the market. This could be as simple as being just 1% better than your competitors.

Don't be afraid of competition. In fact, the presence of competition is a testament to the demand for your product or service. When it comes to competing, you need to strategize improvements to what

your competitors are already doing. This might mean offering excep-tional customer service, unbeatable pricing, or unique products or services. The key is to stand out and be different. Embrace the power of differentiation!

Remember, success isn't about reinventing the wheel. It's about finding opportunities to make small improvements that create a sig-nificant impact. Maybe you offer a new twist on an existing product or a unique experience that customers can't find anywhere else. Whatever it is, make sure it's something that sets you apart from the competition.

Having completed your market research, it's time to put your findings into action and turn your ideas into a concrete plan. It's time to roll up your sleeves and bring your ideas to life. Next we will be turning your market research into a practical plan of action.

Chapter 4

CRAFTING A BLUEPRINT FOR SUCCESS

Writing a business plan can be like trying to bake a cake without a recipe. You know the general ingredients you need, but you're mostly just making educated guesses and hoping for the best outcome. Instead of stressing over every detail, focus on answering these key questions:

> How much money do I need to cover my cost?' and 'Is there enough demand for my product to turn a profit?'

Writing down your thoughts and objectives will help you outline the steps required to bring your business vision to life. This step will ensure that your business is realistic, achievable and tailored to meet the needs of your target market.

Even the most well thought-out plans can sometimes go astray, so don't get too discouraged if things don't go exactly as planned. The road to success is often dotted with crumbled business plans and half-baked ideas, it's just part of the journey.

Don't over build: When starting a business, it's important to keep in mind what you really need to get started. While it may be tempting to dream big and aim for the latest and greatest, ask yourself what are the minimum things you need to start your company. Focus on the essentials that are necessary to get your product or service off the ground.

Overbuilding your idea before testing it out can really hurt! It's important to start small and test your idea before investing too much time or money. This will allow you to refine your concept and make sure there is a market for your product or service. Focus on the essentials!

HOW TO BUILD A BUSINESS PLAN

1. **Start with the essentials:** Begin by providing an overview of your business, including the product or service you offer and how it meets customer needs.
2. **Differentiate:** Identify what sets your business apart from others and you will use this to develop your brand positioning in the market.
3. **Estimate revenue:** Create a spreadsheet to project sales revenue, based on market research, for your product or service.
4. **Inventory**: Make a comprehensive list of everything you'll need to start your business, separating it into "must-have" and "would like to have" items (e.g., website, vehicles, equipment, inventory, employees, etc.).
5. **Costs:** Calculate the total cost of everything you need by researching and obtaining the most accurate pricing possible, instead of relying on guesswork.
6. **Time**: When you launch your business, how quickly will you begin to earn income? It's common for businesses to require a period of time to establish a client base.

Fantastic! Part one is in the books. Now, it's time for the main event! The moment of truth has arrived where you'll discover if your market research and number crunching have crafted a solid business plan. It's like a high stakes game of financial roulette. Will the numbers add up? Let's find out!

Scan here to download a free worksheet:

Covering Your bases: Starting a business usually involves a financial investment, with some ventures being riskier than others. It's best to have some savings set aside for this journey. But if you're feeling daring and want to be known as "The Man Who Started a Business with Two Dollars in His Pocket," prepare for a bumpy ride. Although not impossible, businesses that fail often do so because of poor planning and a lack of funding. To increase your chances of success, have a solid plan and adequate funding.

With that said, starting a new venture requires a realistic approach. Checking all the boxes and having everything you need to succeed is highly unlikely. Be prepared to make trade-offs and prioritize critical aspects of your plan to achieve your goals. Success often requires being resourceful and making the most of what you have, rather than waiting for perfect conditions or ideal circumstances. Keep your focus on what matters most and be ready to adapt and tackle challenges as they arise.

Starting a business is not just about finances, it also requires emotional and mental stability. It's important to communicate with your loved ones, like a spouse or partner, about your plans and the risks involved. Having a support team can greatly improve your chances of success.

And what if loans are part of your plan? Just turn to chapter 9 for all the information you need. This book is here to help you avoid costly mistakes, not paint rainbows and pretend everything is peachy. We want you to be financially stable, not broke and fabulous!

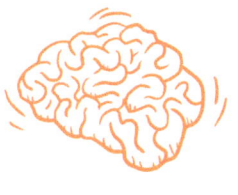

Chapter 5

NAMING YOUR BRAINCHILD

Just like an unborn child, your business is full of potential and possibilities. You have probably spent countless nights dreaming about its future and nurturing it with your hopes and ambitions. I'm sure you have even envisioned what you would name it, giving it a unique identity and personality. Now it's time to bring those dreams to life.

Your business name is important as it will become its identity and set the tone for your brand. Choose a name that's unique and has personality, not too serious or common. The best names are the ones that stand out or have a hint of humor. Don't be afraid to get creative, but make sure it's not too difficult to spell or lengthy. Consider a play on words or pun. After all, your business is your baby. Give it a name that's memorable , just like you want your business to be!

It's time to put those potential business names to the test! Before you make a final decision, it's important to check if any of your competitors have already claimed those names. Simply do a quick Google search and see what comes up. While it's unlikely you'll come up with a completely unique name, it's okay if there are one or two others, as long as they're not in the same service area as you. The goal is to ensure that when your future customers search for your business online, they find you and only you, standing out among the competition.

Make sure your business name isn't already taken or linked to any unsavory controversies or trademarked by someone else. Check out the United States Patent and Trademark Office (USPTO) website to make sure your chosen business name is free and clear to use.

Don't rush this process! Take your time to check the search results thoroughly and avoid any potential legal issues down the line. You want to choose a name that sets a positive tone for your brand and makes a lasting impression on your customers.

Try this name recall exercise: Write down your top 8 name ideas in this book. Tomorrow, without looking, try to recall the names you wrote. If you can't remember them, cross them off your list. If you can't remember the name, chances are your customers won't either. Choose a name that's catchy and easy to remember!

_____   _____

_____   _____

_____   _____

_____   _____

Chapter 6

KING OF YOUR DOMAIN

It's time to tackle the second part of naming your business - securing a suitable URL. Unless you don't plan on having a website, which is unlikely in today's tech-savvy world, it's important to find a suitable URL. Start by checking a website like GoDaddy.com for availability. For most businesses, a .com URL instills confidence in customers.

HOW TO CHOOSE A URL

1. Keep it short and simple. Test it by saying it out loud and asking friends for their opinion.
2. Choose a URL that aligns with your business name and brand identity.
3. Make sure the URL is memorable and easy to spell.
4. Consider the cost of the URL. While you don't need to spend a lot of money, if you find a URL that's perfect for a higher price, it may be worth the investment, especially if you plan to have a significant online presence.
5. Aim for a .com URL as it's more commonly associated with businesses and evokes a sense of credibility.

The different types of domains serve different purposes: .com is commonly used by businesses, .org is specialized for non-profit organizations, .net is intended for companies with a global reach, and .edu is exclusively for educational institutions.

When choosing a URL, ensure to purchase it for a minimum of 3 years. This shows search engines like Google that your business is committed and trustworthy.

The ownership of a URL is public record. However, you don't have to share your personal information with the world. By paying a small fee to your domain provider, they can act as the registrar and keep your information private. This means you won't have to deal with annoying spam calls or emails. You can easily find out who owns a URL by visiting the website "Who Is", where you can get all the juicy details about the website owner. So go ahead, take charge of your domain and keep your privacy intact!

Spicy Tip: Ensure that you register the URL under your own name and account to prevent any future issues with ownership. It's not uncommon for a friend or web developer to register the URL, only for the business owner to lose touch with them and not have a way to claim it. If you lack technical knowledge, seek help, but make sure the URL is registered under your name and account for full ownership and control.

Chapter 7

SUPER AWESOME ENTITIES

Creating a legal structure for your business is like hiring a personal bodyguard to protect both your business and yourself. Sure, it may not be the most thrilling topic, but it's a step you simply cannot skip. But don't worry, I'm going to do my best to make it super awesome for you!

A DBA (Doing Business As) is like having a superhero suit or mask, just like how Peter Parker becomes Spiderman. You can operate under a different name without revealing your true identity, giving you a level of anonymity. This option is perfect for solo entrepreneurs who want to establish a business name without jumping through legal hoops. But just like how a superhero has their kryptonite, a DBA doesn't provide complete protection. Even though you can deposit checks under your business name, all your debts and legal issues will still be linked to your personal social security number. It's important to remember that under that mask, it's still you! Your personal identity and finances are still linked to your business. So if your business gets into trouble, it means you're in trouble too!

Ready to file your DBA? If you're ready to file your DBA (Doing Business As), the process can vary by state, but a simple Google search can guide you in the right direction. You may be able to file at your local or county clerk's office, state agency, or both. Fortunately, the process is generally straightforward and inexpensive.

Limited Liability Company: Also known as a LLC is like having your own an Iron Man suit to protect you from business debts and liabilities. If any problems come up, they have to go through your armor first, giving you peace of mind. And just like Iron Man's suit, an LLC comes with some serious firepower, like pass-through taxation. This means you only have to pay personal income taxes, which is like having a superpower that saves you money! But even superheroes have weaknesses, and an LLC isn't invincible. So, make sure you don't accidentally become the villain! If you engage in any shady or fraudulent activities, the court can still hold you personally liable. Remember to use your powers for good to keep your LLC strong and your assets protected. Another great thing about an LLC is that it gets its own Employment Identification Number (EIN). This is like a social security number but for your business. Your EIN separates your business debts and liabilities from your personal ones, which is like having a secret identity to keep you and your business safe!

You may also want to consider forming an S Corp or a C Corp:

S Corps are like a cool, modified version of LLCs that can have up to 100 shareholders, providing liability protection and tax savings. Meanwhile, C Corps are like the special forces of business formations, offering the highest personal liability protection and the power to raise capital by issuing stocks, although they're subject to double taxation. Just remember to think about your business goals before deciding which one to choose.

This chapter offers only an introduction to the different types of business entities that exist. Please note: Bodyguards and superheroes are not actually provided in practice, and professional guidance should be sought! Moreover, starting small does not constrain your potential for growth. Even starting as a modest DBA, your small business has the potential to thrive and evolve into a prosperous corporation in the future.

HOW TO FILE AN LLC

- **Online Services:** Utilize the services of companies like Legal-Zoom.com or MyCompanyWorks.com to file your LLC. These services are convenient, affordable and take care of the majority of the process for you.
- **Attorney:** Hiring a local attorney can ensure the process is done efficiently and in compliance with state regulations. They can also assist in preparing the articles of organization and operating agreement.
- **Self-filing:** In some states, you can file the LLC on your own by completing the required forms and paying the fees. However, this requires a good understanding of business formation laws and regulations.

Spicy Tip: Once you've filed your LLC, be sure to apply for an EIN (Employer Identification Number) right away. This number is like a social security number for your business and you'll need it to open a business bank account. The good news is, getting an EIN is a free process and can be done in no time. So don't delay, get your EIN as soon as possible to ensure you can easily manage your business finances and keep them separate from your personal finances.

Scan here to apply for an EIN:

Chapter 8

THE BANK BENEFACTOR

As soon as you begin earning or spending money in your business, it is imperative to open a business bank account. This process can be initiated once you have obtained your federal EIN. A business bank account helps you stay legally compliant and protected.

When choosing a bank, consider whether the bank has expertise in your industry. If so, this indicates that the bank offers products and services that are specifically tailored to your business needs.

Smaller banks may be more accommodating to small businesses when it comes to loans. While well-known, large banks may have a strong financial standing and a large marketing budget, they may not be as accessible to small businesses. With a high volume of applicants, these larger banks tend to prioritize those with existing track records, making it difficult for small businesses to secure a loan. At some point you may be looking for capital, and smaller banks may be more open to working with your business and helping you through the loan underwriting process.

As a business owner, developing a strong relationship with your banker is important for the success and growth of your company. A good relationship can secure the necessary funding for starting up or expanding operations, and it can also help to identify the appropriate financial products and services that will enhance the smooth running of your business.

To find the right bank for your business, start by researching and selecting a few potential options. Schedule appointments with their business bankers to have in-depth conversations about your goals and plans. Treat each meeting like a first date, where you both can get to know each other and see if there's a spark. Look for bankers who listen intently, understand your vision, and share your excitement for growth. Take note of the products and services offered by the bank and see which ones align with your needs. It's important to remember that building a strong relationship with your banker takes time and effort, so don't expect a single meeting to win them over completely.

Business bankers are often underappreciated and overlooked as valuable business assets. However, a great banker can prove to be an indispensable partner, serving not only as a source of funding but also as a trusted advisor. Bankers can help guide ambitious entrepreneurs to realistic targets and to growth opportunities.

Honesty is key when it comes to working with your banker. By openly sharing your business challenges, you allow them to identify and match you with the most suitable programs to meet your needs. With their in-depth knowledge, local connections, and ability to offer valuable insights, a good business banker can become a secret weapon in achieving business success.

Chapter 9

OBTAINING LOANS AND CREDIT LINES

You know what they say, "Money talks!" And when it comes to starting a business, having enough cash to get things up and running is necessary. From renting a space to buying equipment and inventory, the costs can quickly add up. But don't let that discourage you! There are plenty of options out there for funding your startup and turning your dreams into a reality. So, let's dive in and explore some of the most popular ways to get the cash you need to kickstart your business.

Bootstrapping: No, this isn't a new dance move. Bootstrapping is when you use your own money to fund your business. It may mean living on ramen noodles for a while, but it's a great way to get started without taking on debt or giving up equity.

Friends and Family: Another option for getting funding for your business is to borrow money from friends and family. This can be a great option if you have people in your life who believe in your idea and are willing to lend you the money you need. However, it's important to approach this option with caution and professionalism. Treat the loan as you would any other business transaction, and make sure to have a written agreement outlining the terms of the loan, including the repayment schedule and interest rate. This can help avoid misunderstandings and potential damage to personal relationships.

Crowdfunding: Have you ever seen a viral crowdfunding campaign and thought, "Hey, I could do that!"? Well, you can! Crowdfunding is when you ask a large group of people to each contribute a small amount of money to fund your project. There are many crowdfunding platforms out there, like Kickstarter and GoFundMe, that can help you get started.

Angel investors: No, these aren't actual angels (although that would be cool). Angel investors are wealthy individuals who invest in startups in exchange for equity. They can be a great source of funding and can also provide valuable mentorship and advice. You can search online for angel investor groups or networks, such as AngelList or Gust, which connect entrepreneurs with investors. It's important to do your research and find investors who are interested in your industry and have experience working with startups.

Venture capital: If you're dreaming big and need a lot of money to get your business off the ground, venture capital might be the way to go. Venture capitalists are investors who provide large sums of money to startups in exchange for equity. But be warned, they often expect a high rate of return on their investment.

Small business loans: If you're not ready to give up equity in your business, a small business loan might be a good option. There are many banks and organizations that offer loans specifically for small businesses. Just be prepared to jump through a few hoops and fill out a lot of paperwork.

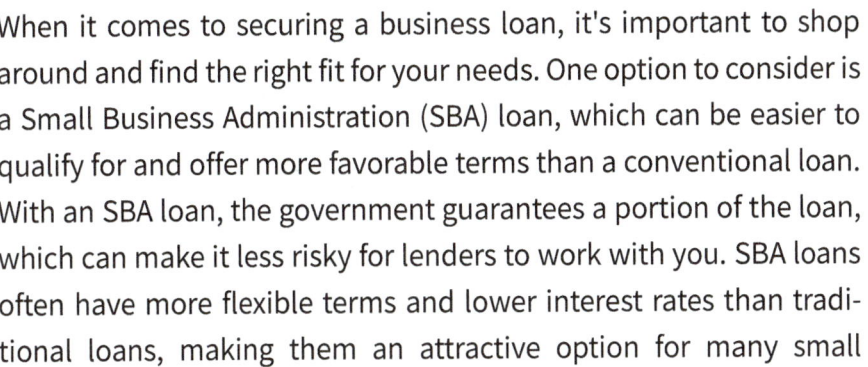

When it comes to securing a business loan, it's important to shop around and find the right fit for your needs. One option to consider is a Small Business Administration (SBA) loan, which can be easier to qualify for and offer more favorable terms than a conventional loan. With an SBA loan, the government guarantees a portion of the loan, which can make it less risky for lenders to work with you. SBA loans often have more flexible terms and lower interest rates than traditional loans, making them an attractive option for many small business owners. However, keep in mind that SBA loans often require a lengthy application process, so be sure to do your research and find a lender that is a good fit for your business.

If you choose to go the conventional route, be prepared to put up collateral, such as property or equipment, to secure the loan. By taking the time to find the right lender and understanding the terms of your loan, you can set your business up for success.

No matter which funding option you choose, remember to do your research and make sure it's the right fit for your business. And don't be afraid to get creative - after all, starting a business is all about taking risks and thinking outside the box!

TIPS FOR GETTING FUNDING

1. **Have a solid business plan:** This is the foundation of your business and should clearly outline your goals, market analysis, financial projections, and other important details.
2. **Prepare financial statements:** You should have a clear understanding of your current financial situation and be able to provide a balance sheet, income statement, and cash flow statement.

3. **Research your funding options:** There are many different types of funding available, including bank loans, angel investors, venture capitalists, and crowdfunding. Research your options and choose the one that best fits your needs.

4. **Build relationships**: Whether you're approaching a bank or an investor, building relationships is key. Networking events and business conferences are great places to meet potential funders.

5. **Be prepared to pitch:** You should be able to explain your business and its potential to potential funders in a clear and concise manner. Practice your pitch until it becomes second nature.

6. **Use video**: Videos are a powerful way to communicate your message and show people what you are working on. Make sure your video is well-produced and engaging.

7. **Be realistic:** Be realistic about your expectations and the amount of funding you need. Overestimating can make you seem unprepared, while underestimating can make you seem unambitious.

8. **Be open to feedback:** Potential funders may have suggestions for improving your business plan or financials. Be open to feedback and be willing to make changes if necessary.

9. **Have a clear repayment plan:** Whether you're taking out a loan or accepting investment, have a clear plan for how you'll pay back the money. This shows that you're responsible and serious about your business.

As you begin the journey of seeking funding for your business, it's important to understand that you'll need to have all your ducks in a row. Have you ever watched Shark Tank? Not every great business idea gets the investors' interest!

One common reason is a lack of preparation. Investors want to see that you have a well-thought-out business plan and a clear vision for how you will use the funds. If you can't articulate your business idea in a compelling way, or if you haven't done the necessary market research, it will be difficult to convince investors to take a chance on you.

Investors and banks want to see that you're committed to your own success. In other words, they want to know that you have some skin in the game. This means that you're willing to invest your own time, money, and resources into your business, not just relying on someone else to foot the bill. So, before you start seeking funding, make sure you have a clear understanding of your financial situation and the amount of capital you're willing and able to contribute. After all, if you're not willing to take a risk on yourself, why should anyone else? Show that you're willing to put in the effort and take on some risk, and investors and banks will be more likely to take a chance on you.

Another reason why potential investors may pass on your business is if you don't have a solid track record. - it's a red flag. Investors want to see that you have a proven track record of success in your industry or relevant experience that makes you qualified to run the business. Plus, your personal finances can also make or break your chances. Do you have legal lawsuits or a bankruptcy in your past? This can be a major turn-off for investors and can seriously hinder your chances of securing funding.

Finally, entrepreneurs may fail to secure funding because they are targeting the wrong investors. It's important to do your research and find investors who are interested in your industry and stage of development. If you're pitching to investors who have no interest in your business, you're wasting your time and theirs.

Despite the challenges, it's important to be patient and persistent. Finding the right investor or bank to fund your business may take time and require a lot of effort. Keep working on your business plan, financials, and other aspects of your business. Don't give up, keep your head up, and keep hustling!

Chapter 10

BUSINESS BUDDY BEWARE

Starting a business can be scary, it's natural to consider bringing in a partner for support and guidance. However, before tying the knot with a business partner, it's wise to take a step back and really get to know them. It's important to assess their strengths, compatibility, and long-term goals before jumping into a grand plan or assigning fancy titles.

Think of it like dating before marriage - you want to make sure your business partner complements your skills, filling in your weaknesses to improve the partnership as a whole. But watch out for the one who lacks actual expertise - there's a big difference between someone who's just excited and someone who knows their stuff like the back of their hand.

Choosing the right business partner is something that requires thought as they will be your co-pilot in making important decisions, creating plans, and sharing responsibilities. Ask yourself, would you trust this person with the most valuable aspects of your life?

Think about it, would you want to go on a vacation with this person? Business, especially entrepreneurship, is a 24/7 job and lifestyle that becomes a part of who you are. You want someone by your side who will support you day and night, hyping you up when you're down and bringing you back to reality when you're feeling too confident. So choose wisely!

Listen to your gut instincts, if you have a nagging feeling that you can't trust this person, consider the cons just as much as the pros. Money has a way of amplifying things and as the dollars start rolling in, who you're seated next to will become amplified too.

Rating your partner

Credit ratings play a major role in choosing a business partner. After all, a strong credit score reflects someone's ability to manage their finances responsibly.

When choosing a business partner, it's imperative to take a look at their credit score and financial history - think of it as a background check before entering a long-term commitment! A healthy credit score shows a person's capability to handle their finances with care, you must have a good understanding of your potential partner's money management skills and views. So, before you commit to a business partnership, make sure to check out your partner's financial history!

Lenders consider the credit scores of anyone who owns more than 20 percent of a business. Having partners with good credit can work wonders for your business. It opens doors for faster and easier access to financing to help you grow and expand your business.

But be wary of partners with poor credit as it can put a damper on your business aspirations. When applying for a business line of credit, banks may require all owners with a significant stake in the business to be listed on the application. And if one of those owners has a blemished credit score, it may result in a denial of your loan request.

Choosing a business partner is an important decision and their personal finances should be taken into consideration, as they can greatly influence the financial future of your business and provide insight into how they will manage the finances of the partnership. Both you and your partner should be open with your finances and your financial standing.

Before you say "I do"

Assess your partner's values. Shared values are key, not just in marriage but in any relationship. Being aligned in ethics and personal principles can ensure a harmonious relationship. Avoid mismatches by ensuring your values align.

Observe your partner's communication style. One way to gauge this is by asking about their past experiences, such as jobs or relationships. If they consistently speak negatively about all their exes, it may indicate an issue with their communication skills and a tendency to place blame on others. This could be a warning sign of potential conflict in the partnership.

Professionalism and vices are not mutually exclusive, and can coexist even in high-powered individuals. Substance abuse, impulsive spending, and gambling are issues that can impact anyone, regardless of their status or position. When considering a potential business partner, examine their personal habits as they can have far-reaching consequences on the success of the enterprise, especially in industries like bars and restaurants where alcohol is a central aspect of the business.

While predicting the future may not be possible, taking the necessary steps to ensure a successful business partnership is definitely within reach. A business partnership can bring together two great minds and provide an opportunity to share the risks and rewards of running a company. Carefully consider what you are looking for in a partner before making a commitment.

If you have decided to say " I do" write down your goals and expectations for the partnership. This could include the role each partner will play in the day-to-day operations of the business, as well as the financial contributions each partner will make. It's also important to assess your own strengths and weaknesses, and consider whether you are looking for a partner who will take an equal role in the business or someone who will take on tasks that are outside of your expertise.

A successful partnership requires clear communication and a shared vision. Disagreements over things like finances or principles can quickly lead to the downfall of the partnership. While the future may be uncertain, taking the time to thoroughly vet a potential business partner and doing your due diligence can go a long way in ensuring the success and longevity of a partnership. By carefully considering your goals, strengths and weaknesses, and by aligning your values, you can increase the chances of forming a successful and long-lasting business partnership.

Despite strong communication and aligned values, all partnerships eventually come to a close. While "till death do us part" may apply to marriages, it is not always the case in business partnerships. In fact, there are a multitude of reasons why a partnership may dissolve, ranging from retirement to career changes, and not always because of a breakdown in relations between partners. To ensure a seamless and hassle-free dissolution process, having a comprehensive exit strategy is imperative. This strategy should include a buy-sell agreement that outlines the conditions for a partner's departure, such as the valuation of privately-held shares, triggers for a buyout, eligible buyers, and the timeline for sales. By having a well-thought-out exit plan in place, both partners can minimize the risk of personal and financial difficulties in the future.

Furthermore, a well-drafted exit strategy can also address other scenarios. For instance, if you or your partner were to go through a divorce, your business assets may become divisible property. Additionally, it is important to consider what will happen in the event of death, and who will inherit the deceased partner's share of the business. It is not enough to only focus on the beginning of the partnership, but it is crucial to also plan for the end. While we hope for a happy retirement with financial security, it's always wise to have contingency plans in place in case things do not go as expected. By anticipating and addressing these potential scenarios, both partners can ensure a smoother and more secure outcome.

Spicy Tip: There's a lot at stake here, which is why it's a good idea to seek legal advice and hire an attorney to help you draft an effective exit strategy. With their expertise, you can ensure that your business is protected and that you're prepared for any eventuality.

Chapter 11

BRANDING MATTERS

Building a brand is like giving your new company a personality! You want to make sure your customers fall head over heels in love with your business. Whether you're going for a modern and sleek look, an eco-friendly vibe, or something a bit more edgy, every aspect of your brand is vital. From the packaging to the office decor, vehicle wraps, and business cards, every detail should be carefully crafted to evoke the feeling you're after. You're not just building a company, you're creating a culture. It's like walking into Starbucks, the dim lighting, the smell of fresh coffee, and the sound of steamers all work together to create a feeling specific to them, or checking into a hotel with a signature scent and feeling like you're already on vacation. Every little detail adds up to create a brand experience that's unforgettable! Branding is more than just a single element, it's the culmination of all the elements that make up your business.

It's a fact of life: most business ideas are simply reincarnations of old concepts with a new twist. However, every now and then a truly original idea comes along. If your big idea has already been explored, don't panic! The solution is to breathe new life into it with smart branding. Get creative and find ways to stand out and make your idea unique.

Before starting your brand-building mission, take a moment to scope out the competition. Think of it as a spy mission, but instead of gathering intel, you're gathering inspiration for your own brand identity. Your goal is to make your new company stand out like a glittering unicorn in a sea of horses - because who doesn't love unicorns? You want to make sure your brand is easily distinguishable from the rest.

Building a strong brand serves as the heart and soul of your organization, shaping audience perception and setting you apart from the competition. So, as you craft your brand, think about what attributes will turn heads and win hearts. What makes your company stand out? What makes it unique and special? These are the elements that will bring your brand to life and help it shine. Your brand is more than just a logo or a catchy tagline. It's the story of your business – your values, your mission, and your purpose!

Your company's core values are another component of your branding strategy. These values, such as empathy, trust, sustainability, speed, and innovation, serve as guiding principles that shape your brand image and influence your customer interactions. Make sure your core values are clearly communicated and integrated into your branding.

With your new company's personality in mind, it's time to start searching for a graphic designer who can bring your vision to life. Remember, a good designer can do more than just create a logo. They're artists, each with their own unique touch. Carefully review the graphic artist portfolio to make sure their style aligns with the brand you have in mind.

When it comes to hiring a designer, you can choose between a famous artist or one who is just starting to develop their skills. The choice often comes down to budget - whether you hire a solo free-lancer or a full-blown design agency, the cost can range from $500 to $10,000.

With so many choices for logo designers, it can be challenging to determine the right one for your needs. However, you can simplify the process by seeking recommendations from fellow business own-ers and investigating local design companies.

When cost is a concern and hiring a designer is not an option, uti-lizing search engines can help you find suitable alternatives. There are numerous online design platforms and international designers, such as Fiverr.com, Etsy.com, or Canva.com, that offer budget-friendly solutions. It's important to keep in mind that opting for a budget-friendly option may result in a logo that resembles someone else's. For small local businesses, this may not pose a problem, but if you're creating a nationally recognized ecommerce brand, it may be worth considering other options.

Don't underestimate the power of a good logo – it's literally the face of your company! It's the first thing people see, and it sets the tone for everything else. It's what makes you stand out in a sea of competition, and it's what makes people say, "Wow, I need to know more about this company!" So, it's worth investing as much as you can in this aspect of your brand. Trust me, a great logo design can do wonders for how people perceive your business.

HIRING A GRAPHIC DESIGNER

1. **Define Your Brand:** Before you start your search, make sure you have a clear understanding of your brand and what you want your logo to represent. Consider your company's mission, values, and target audience.

2. **Do Your Research:** Take the time to research different designers and their portfolios. Look for a style that aligns with your vision and consider the designer's experience and reputation.

3. **Set a Realistic Budget:** Decide on a budget for your logo design and communicate this with your designer. A good logo is an investment that will represent your brand for years to come, so consider spending a bit more for a high-quality design.

4. **Look for Customization:** A custom logo design will set your brand apart and make it unique. Look for a designer who offers custom design services and is willing to work with you to create a unique logo.

5. **Check for Revision Options:** Find out if the designer offers revisions and how many. You want to make sure you are able to make any necessary changes to the design until you are completely satisfied with the final product.

A logo acts as the face of a brand, creating a visual representation that enables people to connect with and remember it. The goal of logo design is to create an emblem that is easily recognizable and evokes memories of experiences with a product, company, or service. A well-designed logo should be simple, memorable, and versatile, reflecting the brand's values and personality in a way that resonates with its audience. When your graphic designer presents you with a few logo options, it's important to keep in mind the key elements that make up a successful logo.

Size: Ensure that your logo is like a chameleon, capable of adapting and looking great in any size or shape. Consider the versatility of logos in locations like Facebook, Instagram, and your company's letterhead. Sometimes, your logo will need to fit into a small square or rectangle. Will it still be legible? Regardless of its size or location, your logo should maintain its allure and charm, regardless of whether it's displayed on a billboard or a business card. In short, make sure your logo is scalable and can fit into any constraint without losing its appeal.

Colors: When it comes to choosing the colors for your logo, it's a balance between looking good and evoking the right emotions in your audience. Opt for 1 to 3 colors, as this range provides the perfect balance between a distinct look and practicality for printing in different forms. Your logo should look just as fabulous in black and white as it does in full color, like the little black dress of branding. Don't be afraid to experiment and ask for multiple color options from your designer. You can even show them off to your friends and have a mini-election to see which colors come out on top in the wild ride of logo color selection!

Design: Simplicity is the name of the logo game! A design that's bold, straightforward, and easy on the eyes will be easier for folks to remember and recognize compared to one that's cluttered and complex. And the cherry on top? A clean logo will keep its cool no matter the size, whether it's mini or mega.

Emblem: Having a logo emblem might not be a must-have, but it can sure come in handy when building your brand identity. Imagine having a tiny picture that instantly pops up on a browser tab, a recognizable icon on your phone app, or the iconic Starbucks logo. That's the kind of impact a logo emblem can have, making your company and brand easily recognizable.

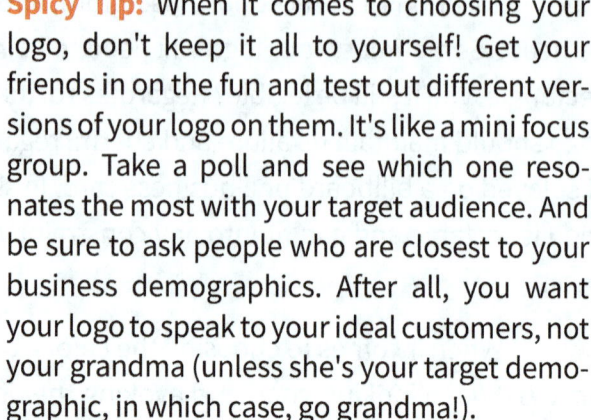

Spicy Tip: When it comes to choosing your logo, don't keep it all to yourself! Get your friends in on the fun and test out different versions of your logo on them. It's like a mini focus group. Take a poll and see which one resonates the most with your target audience. And be sure to ask people who are closest to your business demographics. After all, you want your logo to speak to your ideal customers, not your grandma (unless she's your target demographic, in which case, go grandma!).

As you gear up to receive your new logo, make sure you request all the right files. You will need an EPS file for printing purposes, as well as JPG and PNG versions for digital use. Don't let any unexpected situations catch you off guard, ask for square and rectangular versions too, so your logo can easily fit any shape or space. And don't forget, the original AI file is like the blueprint of your logo, so keep it safe and accessible for any future tweaks or updates.

The journey so far has been amazing, and now with a name and personality for your new company, the future looks even brighter. Get ready for a new chapter filled with endless possibilities. Buckle up, your company is ready to tackle it all!

Chapter 12

WEB WARRIOR

Greetings, fearless web warrior! Well, well, well, looks like a website is a must-have item on every savvy business owner's to-do list! Before you take the first step, take a moment to imagine what you want your website to achieve. Do you see yourself building an online empire, where you can sell your products to the world? Or perhaps you want to showcase your creativity and skills with a portfolio that leaves a lasting impression. Maybe you need a practical solution, like online forms for your patients or contracts for your clients.

And don't forget about the exciting opportunity to offer a membership for exclusive access to your content. Recurring revenue is king! With all these possibilities in mind, take a deep breath and stretch those fingers.

But hold up! Before you dive into building a website, consider whether it's actually necessary for your business. Not every business needs a website, after all. If you're planning to conquer the Amazon marketplace, make a killing in real estate, or become the Etsy craft master of your dreams, a website may not be necessary for your success. If your business doesn't rely on people finding you through search engines, feel free to skip ahead to other important tasks. Remember, a website is not something to jump into without considering its purpose first.

If being found through search engines is a central part of your marketing strategy, a website is a must-have. Think of it as your online headquarters, where all the important information about your business is stored. From your services and pricing, to your contact details and client processes, your website should be the go-to destination for anyone looking to learn more about what you have to offer. When building your website, try not to settle for a generic solution - make sure it's tailored to your specific goals and needs. As your small business grows and evolves, so too will your website, reaching new heights and showcasing your success to the world.

One common mistake is assuming that simply handing over the task of creating a website to a web developer will result in a perfect outcome. While a web developer can certainly bring your ideas to life through programming, they may not have in-depth expertise in your specific industry. If you're looking for a single person to handle all aspects of website creation, such as designing a visually appealing brand, crafting compelling copy, and coding a functional website, you may be disappointed.

This type of project typically requires the collaboration of a team, each with their own specialized skills. If you work with a web design firm, they will have individuals dedicated to each aspect of the project. However, finding a single person who can handle all aspects of website creation is rare. To ensure the best outcome for your website, it's important to understand the roles and responsibilities involved in the process.

If you don't have a team in place, relax, it's OK! Utilize the resources you do have. By this point, you likely have a clear idea of what your branding should look like, including the colors and overall mood you want to convey. This is a great start and an important aspect of your website creation process.

The next step in the website creation process is to have your content ready. If you're selling products, make sure you have high-quality images and descriptions and pricing organized and ready to go. The same applies to any videos and written copy you want to include on your site. Additionally, it's important to have your important pages, such as the contact page and about us page, written and organized in a document. By having these elements in place, you'll be well on your way to creating a comprehensive and effective website.

Spicy Tip: Say "no" to stock images on your website! Using generic images can dilute your brand and fail to convey your unique personality. You can hire a professional photographer, or better yet, tap into the talent of an aspiring photographer in your community. Original, high-quality images on your website are an important aspect of building a strong brand image and can also enhance your website's search engine optimization. Investing in quality images is a small price to pay for the benefits it brings to your brand.

When choosing a web developer, you want to find someone who gets you and can bring your website vision to life. During your initial discussions, make sure you can communicate effectively with your potential developer. If it feels like you're speaking different languages, it's probably not a good sign. You want someone who understands your needs and can offer their expertise to create the website of your dreams. Trust your gut and choose a developer who makes you feel confident and excited about the future of your website.

When you're interviewing web developers, they may start talking about their preferred platforms (don't worry if this sounds like Chinese - we'll dive into that in the next chapter!) and help guide you towards the one that's the perfect fit for your website. Think of it like finding the perfect pair of shoes, but for your website! Some of the most popular platforms out there are WordPress, Wix, and Shopify. But just like shoes, each one has its own strengths and limitations, so it's important to collaborate closely with your developer to figure out which one best aligns with your goals and requirements.

If you're a novice looking to build your own website, fear not! Platforms like WIX, GoDaddy Website Builder, Weebly, and Squarespace are user-friendly and great for those who are new to website building. But just like with anything in life, there's a catch. While these platforms offer the advantage of creating a website on a budget, they do come with some limitations. For example, you'll usually need to pay a monthly fee, and your website can't easily be transferred to a different platform. So if you want to switch things up in the future, you'll need to start from scratch with a new website. Additionally, customization and customer support options can be limited with these platforms. They're often based on drag-and-drop templates and lack advanced features. But hey, if budget constraints are a significant concern, these platforms may provide a great starting point.

Websites come in all shapes and sizes, so don't worry if your budget is tight. What matters most is taking that first step and getting started. Your website could be a traffic-driving machine or a simple online brochure. Whatever it is, make sure it's useful and beneficial

for your customers. The key is to do your best, interview web developers, keep your branding in mind, and create a website that is useful and beneficial for your customers.

WHEN CREATING A WEBSITE

- Consider whether a website is necessary for your business and whether it aligns with your marketing strategy.
- Tailor your website to your specific goals and needs.
- Choose a web developer who understands your needs and can bring your vision to life.
- Communicate effectively with your web developer to ensure you're on the same page.
- Choose a platform that best aligns with your goals and requirements.
- Invest in high-quality, original images that reflect your brand.
- Focus on creating content that is useful and beneficial for your customers.

Chapter 13

THE ANATOMY OF A WEBSITE

If you're not a web expert, no need to stress - that's what the pros are for! However, it's always a good idea to have a basic understanding of how a website works, especially if you're planning on hiring someone to build one for you. So, let's take a minute to dive into the anatomy of a website. You can either take a chance and hope for the best, or get a little bit of knowledge under your belt to make sure you're on the right track. And if you're already a website whiz, then go ahead and skip ahead to the good stuff!

Hosting: When you create a website, all the files that make up your website have to be stored somewhere. Hosting is the service that provides a place for these files to live and be accessible on the internet. Think of it like renting space on the internet to store your website's files. This space is provided by a hosting company, and when someone wants to visit your website, they can type in your website's address and the hosting company will serve up your website's files to their browser. Hosting is like rent. You can't just pay once and forget about it. For as long as your website is up and running, you'll need to keep up with hosting payments.

URL: Let's give it up for the superhero of the web world - the URL Uniform Resource Locator (AKA the domain) It's the thing that people type in to access your website, like yourcompanyname.com. Your Domain name puts a friendly face on hard-to-remember numeric internet addresses - it's something that belongs to you (as long as you pay for it). Just like hosting, when you register a domain, it's yours to keep (or lose, if you forget to renew it).

Now, here's where things get really cool. Every computer on the internet has a unique internet protocol (IP) number. But, no one wants to remember a bunch of numbers to access their favorite websites. That's where domain names come in! They put a friendly face on those hard-to-remember numeric addresses. For example, instead of typing in the IP number for whitehouse.gov (which is 104.109.178.94), you can just type in the easy-to-remember domain name, whitehouse.gov. Cool, huh?

The internet is your oyster when it comes to registering your URL! There are so many places where you can claim your very own domain name, like Domain.com, Google Domains, Dreamhost, and GoDaddy. It's like a smorgasbord of options! So, take your pick and make your mark on the world wide web. Just remember, with great domain names comes great responsibility!

HTTPS: (Hypertext Transfer Protocol Secure) is a way of securing the communication between a website and its users. It provides an extra layer of security, making it harder for hackers to intercept any sensitive data being transmitted, such as passwords or credit card information.

Have you ever been to a website and seen the dreaded message, "Not secure"? It's not necessarily a sign that there's a hacker lurking around every corner. It just means that the website doesn't have an SSL (Secure Sockets Layer) certificate installed on its server.

So, what is an SSL certificate, you ask? It's a small data file that verifies the identity of your website and creates a secure connection between your website and your visitors' web browsers. When you see a website URL that starts with "https://" instead of "http://", that means the site has an SSL certificate and any information you enter is encrypted, making it much harder for hackers to steal or intercept it.

Spicy Tip: SSL certificates aren't very expensive - usually around $150 a year - and they're even free if you're a tech whiz. But, for most of us mere mortals, it's easier to just pay the money and move on. While having a secure site isn't strictly necessary, it does help build trust with your visitors and can even improve your website's ranking on search engines. So, don't be caught with your website security down - get that SSL certificate installed and keep your visitors' data safe and sound!

Platforms: The world's very first website went live on August 6, 1991. That wasn't all that long ago! Since then, we've come a long way in terms of creating websites. Nowadays, we have a whole buffet of options when it comes to building a website. But, just like choosing the foundation of your home, choosing the right website builder (aka website platform) is crucial. It will determine everything from the look and feel of your site to how easy it is to maintain, add on to, and more.

Luckily, your web developer has got your back and can help guide you in making the right choice. There are many website platforms to choose from, each with their own unique strengths and weaknesses. Some are better suited for e-commerce, while others are great for content creation or creating membership pages. WordPress, Drupal,

Magento, Joomla, Weebly, and Shopify are just a few of the most popular website builders out there.

When choosing a website builder, it's generally recommended to go for one with a CMS (content management system). This will make it easier for you to control and edit your site, and add on to it as your business grows.

Don't get overwhelmed by the options out there - take your time and find a website platform that works for you and your business. With the right tools at your fingertips, you'll be well on your way to creating a website that's just as awesome as you are!

Themes: If you're looking to create a website quickly and cost-effectively, website themes are your go-to solution. A website theme is a pre-designed template that you can use as a foundation for your site. Most every platform has themes. There are thousands of themes available, both free and paid, and you can find them on websites like https://themeforest.net. They offer themes for almost every type of website you can think of, from business to entertainment and everything in between.

The great thing about website themes is that they control the overall design of your website. You don't have to worry about starting from scratch or designing everything yourself. With a theme, you can customize the look and feel of your website to fit your brand, and you'll be up and running in no time.

So, be sure to ask your web developer about website themes and see if they have any recommendations. With a little research and some creativity, you'll be able to find the perfect theme for your website and create a stunning online presence.

Well, that's a wrap, folks! I know the topic might not be the most thrilling, but having a basic understanding of website building is definitely not a waste of brain space. Understanding the fundamentals can help you make informed decisions, communicate more effectively with your web developer, and save you some headaches down the road.

Who knows, you might have even discovered a new passion! Plus, impressing your friends with your newfound web knowledge isn't too shabby either.

Chapter 14

MARKETING NAVIGATOR

Marketing has been around for centuries, with clever packaging and language being used to sell everything from potions to goods. The term "marketing" is believed to have originated in Europe in the early 1500s, when traveling merchants sold their wares at town markets. But while the goal of marketing has remained the same over time - to deliver the right message to the right person at the right time - the methods have evolved. In the past, companies relied on old-school methods like billboards and flyers to reach potential customers.

Have you ever noticed how many companies have names that start with A1? It's not because they lack imagination; it's because they wanted to be the first listing in the phone book. Yes, the phone book, that thick stack of paper that we used to use before Google Maps. And since the letter A was at the top of the list, businesses figured that naming themselves A1 would give them a leg up. It was the ultimate marketing hack, and it worked like a charm. So the next time you're thumbing through an old phone book, remember that those A1 businesses were the original pioneers of search rankings.

It's no secret that Google is an incredible tool, and ranking at the top of its search results can do wonders for your business. You'd be on your way to taking over the world! However, if you're starting something like a t-shirt company, it's important to keep in mind that the competition is fierce. With hundreds of thousands of pages vying for the top spot, the chances of your website beating out the competition are slim. It's like trying to win a game of musical chairs when there are a hundred other players and only one chair. In order to succeed, you'll need a strategic and realistic plan for getting to the top of the search results. Otherwise, you'll just end up spinning your wheels and getting nowhere fast.

SEO: (Search Engine Optimization) is like a game where you try to make your website rank higher on Google, and Google uses a complex algorithm to decide which websites to show first. But with the rise of AI, the game is getting tougher. AI-powered algorithms can now better understand what users want, making it harder to manipulate rankings with traditional SEO tactics. In fact, AI is evolving rapidly and may even allow other search engines to compete with Google in the future. So, it's more important than ever to focus on creating high-quality, user-focused content that adds value and meets the needs of your audience to stay ahead in the game.

One effective strategy for success in business is to create niche markets. Instead of targeting broad categories like "t-shirts," focus on more specific markets such as "gothic t-shirts." By doing so, it becomes easier to stand out and rank highly in search results.

Whether you're in a product or service industry, finding a niche and becoming an expert in that area can be highly beneficial. For example, Roto-Rooter started out as a regular plumbing company, but they were able to pivot and rebrand themselves as experts in drain services. By specializing in one area, they were able to corner that

particular market and build a strong reputation and branding for themselves.

In a service industry, becoming an expert in a particular field can also help you to differentiate yourself from competitors. This can involve developing specialized skills or knowledge, or simply focusing on one particular aspect of your business. By doing so, you can attract a specific audience and position yourself as a go-to expert in your field.

Focusing on a specific niche also has significant advantages from a cost perspective. When you market to a niche, you face less competition, which can lead to lower costs per ad and higher conversion rates. By targeting a specific audience, you can create more targeted and effective marketing campaigns.

To succeed in business, you must first identify your target market and devise a solid plan to convert them into loyal customers. Rather than trying to be everywhere, focus on being where it matters most.

For instance, if Nike started selling their products at the dollar store, it would be a recipe for disaster. It's important to maintain the integrity of your brand and reputation by carefully selecting the channels through which you market your product or service. This means choosing the right platforms, locations, and marketing channels that align with your brand and reach your target audience effectively.

Google Maps: Planning to sell products or services locally? Google Maps is about to become your new BFF (best friend forever). By creating a Google Maps listing at business.google.com, you can attract more local customers to your business.

To make your listing stand out, take the time to upload high-quality pictures, properly categorize your business, and gather lots of customer reviews. Did I mention reviews? Yes, lots and lots of them!

The more reviews you have, the more likely people are to choose your business over others.

By utilizing Google Maps, you can improve your local search visibility and make it easier for potential customers to find you. With over a billion active users, Google Maps is a powerful tool for reaching a wider audience and growing your business. So, take the time to optimize your listing and reap the benefits of being a top-rated business on Google Maps.

Adwords: AdWords is like having your own personal genie in a bottle for online advertising - it grants your wish of reaching a wider audience through pay-per-click (PPC). It's exactly what it sounds like - you create an ad, choose a relevant keyword, and whenever someone types that keyword into Google and clicks on your ad, you pay for that click. It's a bit like the magic lamp in Aladdin, but instead of rubbing it, you're typing in a keyword. With AdWords, you can target specific keywords that are relevant to your business, and show your ads to the people who are most likely to convert into customers.

But, beware my friend - this genie has a dark side! It's like Jekyll and Hyde of online advertising. It's REALLY easy to overspend and get minimal results if you're not careful. While Google offers free services to help you set up ads, watch out for the "helpful" phone reps who may not understand your market. Don't let your AdWords wishes become nightmares! Consider outsourcing the work or hiring an expert. It may be an additional cost, but having someone who understands your business and target audience is generally a good investment. Upwork.com and Fiverr.com are great places to find talented professionals who can help you achieve your goals.

There are several types of AdWords campaigns that you can run to promote your business, like the superheroic Display Network, the savvy Search Network, and the stealthy Remarketing campaign. With these powerful tools in your utility belt, you can bring in customers faster than a speeding bullet. Let's go save the day and your marketing budget!!

Alright, let's put the puns aside and get back to business. I must confess, I got a little carried away there. We've had our fun, and now it's time to focus on what really matters.

TYPES OF ADWORDS CAMPAIGNS

- **Search Network Campaigns:** These campaigns are designed to show your ads to people who are actively searching for the products or services you offer on Google Search.
- **Display Network Campaigns:** These campaigns allow you to show your ads on websites, videos, and mobile apps that are part of Google's Display Network.
- **Shopping Campaigns:** These campaigns are used for e-commerce businesses that want to promote their products on Google Shopping, which is a search engine specifically for online shopping.
- **Video Campaigns:** These campaigns promote your video ads on YouTube and across the Google Display Network.
- **App Campaigns:** These campaigns are designed to promote your mobile app across Google Search, Google Play, YouTube, and the Google Display Network.
- **Local Campaigns:** These campaigns are designed to drive foot traffic to your physical store. Your ads will show up on Google Search, Google Maps, and other Google platforms.

Choosing the right campaign type depends on your target market and budget. This is a complex topic, and like all marketing, the content you create plays a significant role. It's important to AB test your campaigns to determine what performs best. Simply getting clicks won't necessarily generate revenue, so you must focus on attracting leads that convert into paying customers. If you're not an expert in this field, you have two options: A) learn more about it, or B) hire a professional. Taking a haphazard approach can lead to unsuccessful campaigns, resulting in higher costs than investing in a professional from the outset.

YouTube: Welcome to the world of YouTube - a platform that's exceptional for businesses to advertise and connect with a vast audience of viewers. It's not just a platform for cat videos and makeup tutorials, no sir! YouTube really lets you put your personality into things, and its diverse audience allows people to showcase their uniqueness. Plus, it's an amazing way to generate brand awareness and expand your reach. Now, it's worth noting that conversion rates tend to be lower on YouTube compared to other platforms, but don't you worry!

We've all experienced the frustration of waiting to skip an ad before watching our desired video. To make an impact on this platform, create ads that are so captivating that viewers forget all about the video they intended to watch and get lost in your ad instead. This requires focusing on creating engaging and visually appealing content that resonates with your target audience.

TIPS FOR YOUTUBE ADS

1. **Know your audience:** Before creating your ad, make sure you have a clear understanding of your target audience. What are their needs, wants, and pain points? What kind of content do they typically engage with on YouTube?
2. **Keep it short and sweet:** Attention spans are short, so try to keep your ads under 30 seconds if possible. Get straight to the point and make your message clear and compelling.

3. **Grab their attention early:** In the first few seconds of your ad, make sure to grab the viewer's attention and entice them to keep watching. Use a catchy headline, engaging visuals, or an intriguing story to pique their interest.

4. **Show, don't tell:** Rather than just talking about your product or service, show it in action. Use visuals to demonstrate how it works and how it can benefit the viewer.

5. **Include a clear call-to-action:** Make it easy for viewers to take action by including a clear call-to-action at the end of your ad. This could be to visit your website, sign up for a free trial, or buy your product.

6. **Test and analyze your ads:** Use A/B testing to see which ads are performing best and analyze your ad metrics to measure your success. Use this information to make improvements and optimize your future ads.

Creating videos and a channel for free is definitely an option if you're looking to attract organic traffic or potentially go viral. However, let's delve further into this topic in the social marketing section.

Email Marketing: Email marketing can be a bit of a puzzle. On one hand, you've got a direct line to your customers' inboxes. But what do you even say? And how often is it too often to hit 'em up? And where do you even get all those emails in the first place? It's like solving a tricky riddle. Here are some tips to help you crack the code!

First things first, let's agree not to spam people who aren't interested in our emails. Nobody likes that. Instead, focus on building a high-quality email list of people who have given you permission to contact them. A great way to do this is by using the 'ole coupon trick' as my daughter likes to call it! This is where you offer something valuable in exchange for their email address. It could be a discount on their first purchase, early access to exclusive products, or even free content. Remember, people won't give you their email just because you ask for it. You need to give them a good reason to sign up.

The second piece of the email marketing puzzle is creating some killer content! And lucky for us, there are some seriously awesome email marketing software programs out there to help us get the job done. You've got your Mailchimp, Constant Contact, Aweber, Hub-Spot and more!

Think of these programs like having a personal assistant who takes care of all the behind-the-scenes work, so you can focus on creating great content and connecting with your audience. They help you manage your email lists, design and send newsletters, and track your campaign's success.

But here is the thing - you can't just send out the same email to everyone on your list. That's a recipe for disaster! Instead, you've gotta get specific. Let's say someone signs up for your email list. You can tell your email program to add some tags to their profile, based on their purchases, preferences, and likes. This allows you to send emails that are tailored to each individual's interests. After all, you wouldn't want to send a cat food email to a dog owner, would you?

The more granular you can get with your email targeting, the better. By sending content that's relevant and interesting to each person on your list, you'll increase engagement, boost conversions, and create raving fans who can't wait to hear from you again. So get specific, get targeted, and get ready to see some serious results!

When it comes to crafting your email campaigns, remember that people are BUSY. They don't have time for fluff or nonsense. So, get straight to the point and don't overwhelm them with too much info. Spice things up with some images that'll break up the text and keep 'em engaged. And please, please, please include a clear call-to-action! Otherwise, they'll just be left hanging like a piñata without a stick.

When you launch your first email marketing campaign, keep a close eye on the numbers. Check out your email analytics to see how many people are opening your emails, clicking on links, and taking action. If you're not seeing the results you want, don't give up! Try testing different email subject lines or types of content to see what resonates with your audience. And don't forget the basics, like proof-reading and grammar! You don't want to end up sending out an email with a typo. It's time to make your English teacher proud!

SMS: (Text Message Marketing) can be a powerful tool for businesses to reach and engage with their target audience. SMS messages have an impressive open rate and are often read within minutes of being received, making them an effective way to quickly and directly communicate with customers. However, the effectiveness of SMS marketing depends on a variety of factors, including your target audience, industry, and marketing goals.

For businesses that have a well-defined target audience and a clear strategy for delivering value through SMS messages, such as appointment reminders, loyalty programs or exclusive flash sales, SMS marketing can be a valuable tool. However, it's important to note that SMS messages are not typically effective for general product promotion or informational purposes.

As with any marketing strategy, it's important to evaluate the effectiveness of SMS marketing for your business on an ongoing basis and adjust your approach as needed. By focusing on delivering value and relevance to your target audience through SMS, you can create a successful and engaging marketing campaign that drives results.

TIPS FOR SMS MARKETING

1. **Get permission:** Always make sure you have the recipient's permission before sending SMS messages. This will help you avoid complaints and legal issues down the line.

2. **Keep it short and sweet:** SMS messages have a character limit, so it's important to keep your messages concise and to the point. Focus on the key message you want to communicate and avoid unnecessary details.

3. **Personalize your messages:** Use the recipient's name and any other relevant information you have to personalize your messages. This will help you build a stronger connection with your audience and increase engagement.

4. **Time your messages:** Timing is key when it comes to SMS marketing. Avoid sending messages during early morning hours or late at night when people are more likely to be asleep. Instead, send messages during business hours when people are more likely to be checking their phones.

5. **Include a clear call to action:** Every SMS message should include a clear call to action. Whether it's asking the recipient to make a purchase, visit your website, or sign up for a newsletter, a clear and specific call to action can improve conversion rates.

6. **Provide value:** Offer exclusive promotions, discounts, or other incentives that are only available to SMS subscribers. This will encourage people to sign up and stay engaged with your brand.

7. **Test and analyze your campaigns:** Continuously test and analyze your SMS campaigns to see what works and what doesn't. Use A/B testing to test different message formats, calls to action, and other elements to optimize your campaigns for better results.

Direct Mail: Direct mail marketing might seem like a thing of the past, but it's still alive and kickin'! In fact, it's a highly effective way to reach customers and drive results for your business.

DIRECT MAIL BENEFITS

- **High response rates:** Believe it or not, direct mail marketing still gets better response rates than emails and other digital marketing channels. Direct mail response rates tend to vary from 1% to over 5%.
- **Tangibility and personalization:** Direct mail marketing is like a love letter in the mail, only it's from your favorite business! When customers receive a physical piece of mail, they feel like they're getting something special. And with the power of personalization, businesses can send customers something they'll love!
- **Less competition:** You know how your inbox is full of emails from businesses trying to get your attention? Well, the mailbox is a lot less crowded. That means your direct mail piece has a better chance of standing out and getting noticed. It's like being the cool kid at the party with no competition.
- **Trust and credibility:** Direct mail marketing can help businesses build trust and credibility with their customers. A physical piece of mail shows that a business is willing to invest time and resources to connect with its customers. It's like getting a handwritten note from your grandma!
- **Integration with digital marketing:** Direct mail marketing can be integrated with digital marketing to create a powerful and fun marketing strategy. For example, businesses can include QR codes on their direct mail pieces to drive customers to their website or social media channels.

When it comes to direct mail, the package counts! Opt for things like colorful envelopes, hand-written fonts for the address, and first-class stamps. These little touches can increase the likelihood that someone will open your letter and engage with your message.

Direct mail can also be a powerful way to make your customers feel special. Whether it's sending birthday cards or exclusive invites to your events, direct mail lets you connect with your customers on a personal level.

So don't dismiss direct mail as a thing of the past. With a little bit of creativity and some thoughtful touches, you can use direct mail to stand out and deliver your message in a way that truly resonates with your customers.

Events: Who doesn't love a good party? It's the perfect way to bring your tribe together and get to know each other over some delicious snacks and drinks. I call this marketing strategy "the hot dog trick".

It all started a few years ago when a fancy speaker store was having a sale. But instead of flashy ads and promotions, they decided to go with a grill and some hot dogs. And you know what? The parking lot was packed! My friend, who just wanted a tasty hot dog, ended up leaving with thousands of dollars worth of Sono speakers. And he wasn't the only one! There's just something about a gathering that puts people at ease and makes them more likely to connect with your business.

So why not throw a party for your tribe? It doesn't have to be anything fancy - just a chance for people to come together and have some fun. And who knows? You might just end up with some new customers or clients. It's like having your cake and eating it too!

Events are a fantastic way to create content and engage with your customers. They're like a treasure trove of photo opportunities that you can use to promote your brand on various platforms, from email and social media to YouTube and beyond.

But the benefits of events go way beyond just capturing some great shots. They're also an opportunity to connect with your customers on a deeper level and build a sense of community around your brand. Nobody likes to party alone - events are a chance to bring people together and make new connections.

And let's not forget the power of like-mindedness. When people come together at your event, they're surrounded by others who share their values and interests. It's like a magnet for people who are looking for connection and community, which can be a powerful driver for your brand.

Events can be a powerful addition to your marketing strategy. Whether you're launching a new product or celebrating the holidays, events provide endless opportunities for creating memorable experiences for your customers. Plus, you might just make some new friends and fans along the way!

And it's not just about having a good time - events also give you the chance to engage with your customers and receive valuable feedback. It's like a direct line to their thoughts and feelings, which can help you improve your brand and marketing efforts.

So why not fire up the grill, pour some drinks, and get this party started? A fun and engaging event can have a huge impact on your business, and you never know what kind of connections you might make. It's time to grab a hot dog and see what happens!

Chapter 15

THE SOCIAL MEDIA METHOD

O K, you know yourself better than anyone else. So, before diving headfirst into social media marketing, it's important to be brutally honest with yourself about your social media skills. If you're not a social media person, and you're planning to manage your social media presence on your own, it's time to think twice. A poorly managed social media page can do more harm than good.

For some businesses, social media is a must, especially if your mission is to succeed through brand awareness or word of mouth. If you're just starting out, social media can be an excellent tool to connect with your audience, build a community, and promote your business. But, if you're a proctologist, for example, a Google Map with good reviews may be all you need to attract new patients.

To truly dominate social media, you've got to bring creativity and originality. You can't just rely on sharing your friend's hilarious cat memes and generic stock photos – that's so last decade! You need to step up your game with fresh, engaging content that's tailor-made for your audience. Whether it's stunning photos or killer sales messages, you need to give it all you've got to stand out from the crowd in the social media world and give your audience something to talk about!

Social media is a vast and varied landscape, with many platforms to choose from. You've got the big guns like Facebook, Instagram, Twitter, LinkedIn, YouTube, TikTok, Snapchat, and Pinterest, just to name a few. Which platforms you choose to focus on will depend on your specific market and marketing strategy. If you're looking to streamline your social media management, there are tools available that allow you to post to multiple platforms simultaneously. Check out some of these options, like Brandwatch, Loomly, Sendible, Hootsuite, and Sprout Social.

With these tools, you can easily create and schedule posts for multiple social media platforms all in one place. This saves you time and energy, allowing you to focus on creating amazing content that resonates with your audience.

Plus they offer robust analytics and reporting features, allowing you to measure the success of your campaigns. You can see how your posts are performing, track your brand's reputation, and gain insights into your audience's demographics, interests, and behavior.

Different social media platforms have different audiences and content styles. For example, Twitter is known for its short, snappy updates and breaking news, while Instagram is all about visual content and aesthetically pleasing feeds. Make sure you're creating content that's well-suited to the platform you're using. If you're not sure which platforms are best for your content, try experimenting with a few to see what resonates with your audience.

Building a relationship with your audience is key to building momentum and increasing the chances of your content getting shared. Respond to comments and messages, ask for feedback, and use your social media channels to create a sense of community around your brand or content. This can help build loyalty and a sense of ownership among your followers, making them more likely to share your content with their own networks.

When it comes to social media, there are plenty of pros out there who can help you reach your goals. Whether it's a professional agency or your tech-savvy teenage niece, the choice ultimately depends on your budget and what you're trying to achieve in the social media world. It's important to consider what level of expertise you need and what resources you have available before making a decision.

Here's a few tips:

First off, be timely and relevant. Jump on trends and current events, and put your own unique spin on it. Make sure your content is shareable and easy to digest - no one wants to read a novel on their Instagram feed. Use eye-catching visuals and snappy captions to grab people's attention.

Don't be afraid to take risks and push boundaries - just make sure you're staying true to your brand and values. And always engage with your audience and respond to comments and messages. Building a genuine connection with your followers can lead to increased engagement and, who knows, maybe even a shot at viral fame.

Building a following on social media can be tough. But it's OK, there's no need to resort to buying friends or likes. Instead, consider investing in targeted advertising on social media platforms. Whether you want to promote your website, showcase a new product, or simply boost engagement on a post, social media advertising can help you reach your target audience and grow your following over time. With a little strategy and patience, you can build a strong tribe of engaged followers who genuinely connect with your brand.

At the end of the day, don't put all your eggs in the viral basket. Building a solid, engaged community takes time and effort, but it's a more sustainable approach for long-term success. So keep creating great content, engaging with your audience, and who knows, maybe one day you'll be the next internet sensation.

Going Viral

Going viral on social media is like winning the lottery - it's rare! Sure, it's fun to dream of instant internet fame and glory, but the reality is that building a strong brand and loyal following is a more reliable strategy for long-term success. But hey, if you're feeling lucky, there are some ways to increase your chances.

If you're really serious about trying to go viral, it may be worth investing in influencer marketing or paid promotion. Influencers with large followings can help give your content a boost, while targeted ads can help you reach a wider audience. Just be sure to choose influencers or ad platforms that are well-aligned with your brand and content.

And finally, the most important tip of all: have fun with it! If you're not enjoying the process, your audience will be able to tell. So, let loose, be silly, and remember that sometimes, the best things in life are the ones that make us laugh.

Remember, going viral is never a guarantee, and it's not the only measure of success on social media. Building a loyal following and creating valuable content that resonates with your audience is the foundation for long-term success. But by following these tips and putting in the effort, you just might hit that viral jackpot. And if you do go viral, don't forget to send me a virtual high-five.

Chapter 16

GETTING REVIEWS

Gathering reviews is like throwing a party - the more people you invite, the better it gets. We've all heard the phrase, "The more, the merrier," and I think the saying applies perfectly here!

First things first, make sure your customers can find you. Let's put ourselves in their shoes - they just had an amazing experience with your business and want to tell the world about it. So, provide them with some options! You can create a website, set up some social media profiles, or list yourself on review sites like Yelp or Google My Business. The more options you give, the easier it is for customers to find you and leave a review.

But what about negative reviews? Don't worry, it's not the end of the world. Think of it as a friendly reminder to improve your product or service. Take a deep breath, read the review carefully, and see how you can make things better. You can even reach out to the customer to offer a solution or make things right. Who knows, they may even change their review to a positive one!

HOW TO GET REVIEWS

1. **Ask your customers:** You can simply ask your customers to leave a review on your website or on a review site like Yelp or Google Reviews. You can do this in person, via email or social media, or even with a printed request on a receipt or in your store.

2. **Incentivize your customers**: You can offer a discount, coupon, or other incentive for customers who leave a review. Be careful not to offer incentives in exchange for positive reviews, as this can violate the terms of service of some review sites.

3. **Incentivize employees:** Since you may be busy running your business, incentivizing your team to ask customers for reviews can be helpful. Get creative with your incentives-consider running a friendly competition and offering a prize to the employee with the most reviews, or provide a per-review bonus to all employees. You can also make it a team effort, setting a goal for a certain number of reviews and offering a reward once that goal is achieved. The more enthusiastic your employees are about obtaining reviews, the more likely you are to receive them!

4. **Use an automated review request system:** You can use a service like Podium or Birdeye to automate review requests and follow-ups with customers who have recently made a purchase or used your service.

5. **Partner with influencers:** If you have a product, you can partner with influencers in your niche to review your product and share their thoughts with their audience.

6. **Provide excellent customer service:** By providing excellent customer service, you can increase the chances that your customers will leave a positive review. Responding quickly to customer inquiries and resolving issues can help encourage positive reviews.

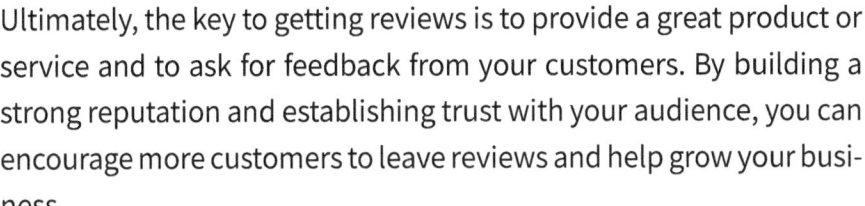

Ultimately, the key to getting reviews is to provide a great product or service and to ask for feedback from your customers. By building a strong reputation and establishing trust with your audience, you can encourage more customers to leave reviews and help grow your business.

When it comes to crafting your review pages, don't rush through it. Take the time to ensure that all the information you include is accurate and up-to-date. This will help you build trust with potential customers and establish your credibility.

To make your review pages more appealing, add some eye-catching images that showcase your products or services. It's also important to include an "About Us" section that gives customers a taste of your business's unique flavor. And don't forget to provide all the contact information customers could want, like your store hours and phone number.

Claim your business on popular directories like Google, Yelp, and Facebook. Some pages allow you to create a vanity URL, which will help customers find you more easily and give you more visibility online. Remember, to get love, you have to show love. So put some love into your review pages! They're a reflection of your business, and a little TLC can go a long way in attracting new customers.

Chapter 17

FINDING A TRIBE

Truth bomb here: not everyone will be a fan of your brand and business, and that's completely fine. Instead of trying to win over the entire world, concentrate on creating a passionate fanbase. Seek out those who share your values, who are eager to become avid supporters of your brand, and who will wholeheartedly embrace everything you have to offer. Attempting to please everyone is a surefire way to failure. You'll end up with a bland, unappetizing brand that's hard to swallow

If you're doing things right, you'll definitely encounter some criticism. Some may think your product is too cheap, others may think it's too expensive. It's too big, it's too small. The list goes on. But, don't let the naysayers get you down. Keep your values front and center. They'll help you stay focused and maintain clarity in your vision and mission. Don't dilute your brand by trying to please everyone. Stand firm in your convictions, and you'll have a business that's truly worth bragging about!

Building a fan club should be part of the business plan. Create a community of people who are passionate about what you stand for.

This is what owning a business is all about - creating a tribe of supporters who love what you have to offer.

You want to create something that will have people talking. We all check reviews before making a purchase, share our thoughts on social media, and tell our friends and co-workers about our latest finds. We're all influencers in our own right, from the clothes we wear to the cars we drive. We're constantly building our own communities and tribes.

By now, you've done your homework. You know who your target market is. The next step is to turn those people into your tribe. Create a brand that speaks to them, that resonates with their values and desires. Connect with them on a deeper level and show them that you understand them. When you do this, you'll have a tribe that's fiercely loyal and always eager to spread the word about your brand.

And you might be wondering, "How do I do that?" Well, it's actually super simple! Just ask! And when they do, show your appreciation and gratitude. You can reward your tribe with gifts or simple gestures of thanks. Every person your business interacts with has the potential to become a promoter through a great review or referral. So, don't be shy, ask for their support!

Chapter 18

TURNING CUSTOMERS INTO MEMBERS

L et's talk about recurring income - the kind of money that keeps flowing into your pockets like a never-ending stream of cash. And if you do a good job, you can count on it every month or year, like clockwork.

Subscriptions and membership programs are amazing things. And guess what? Most any business, services or products, can bring in this sweet, sweet dough by being a little creative and offering a membership service.

Here is an example: Let's say you run an HVAC company. What if you offered your customers a bi-annual machine tune-up for a reasonable price?

Not only would you be raking in that recurring income, but you'd also be making contact with your customers twice a year. This means you'll be building a strong relationship with them, and they'll see you as the go-to HVAC company for all their needs.

And what about slow months? By offering this kind of service, you'd have guaranteed work on the horizon! Plus, if your customers need repairs or a brand new unit, they'll be ringing your phone off the hook, thanks to the trust and loyalty you've built with them.

Get creative and brainstorm some ideas for membership perks! How about exclusive discounts, early access to new products or services, or a VIP customer service line?

THE THREE ESSENTIAL C'S

1. **Cash flow:** With enough recurring income, you can cover your expenses and put your company on some seriously stable ground.
2. **Customer loyalty:** By becoming the go-to provider for whatever you're selling, you'll build strong relationships with your customers and keep them coming back for more.
3. **Capital Assets:** Offering a membership service can increase the value of your company if you ever decide to sell it, as potential buyers will see the value in your loyal members.

Setting up a membership program is actually pretty easy! The secret is to use specialized invoicing programs like FreshBooks, Square, or Keap, which can take care of all the administrative tasks for you.

These programs offer tons of features that go beyond just invoicing and credit card charging, including sending out payment reminders to ensure that you get paid on time. This means you can focus on building strong customer relationships and delivering excellent service to your members without getting bogged down in paperwork.

Offering a membership service could be just the thing you need to improve your cash flow, boost customer loyalty, and increase the overall value of your company.

So, now it's time to put on your thinking cap and brainstorm some ideas for your own membership program. Take a moment and start jotting down some ideas and see how a membership program can take your business to the next level!

Need help with ideas? The best way to generate ideas is by brainstorming with friends and colleagues. Gather a group of people and start discussing potential membership perks, benefits, and rewards that would appeal to your customers. Think outside the box and don't be afraid to get creative!

Start by jotting down some ideas while answering two key questions.

First, consider what benefits your customers will receive from the membership program. Whatever it may be, make sure it's a clear and compelling benefit that will entice customers to sign up.

Second, think about how the membership program will benefit your business. Will it increase customer loyalty and retention, provide a steady stream of recurring revenue, or give you valuable insights into your customers' preferences and behaviors? Be sure to consider how the program fits into your overall business strategy and goals.

Based on your responses, you can create a membership program that is both beneficial to your customers and your business.

Chapter 19

THE PROCESSING PLAN

Making money is the goal of every business, and accepting payments is a key part of achieving this. Choosing the right credit card processor can have a significant impact on your sales and keep your customers happy by providing fast, secure, and convenient payment options.

Merchant services providers act as the middleman between your business and financial institutions, offering a variety of hardware, software, and financial services to help you process credit and debit card transactions quickly and efficiently. These services, whether it's a credit card terminal or an online payment gateway, can make it easier for you to get paid and keep your customers satisfied.

When it comes to choosing the right merchant services provider, shop around for the best deal. Fees can vary based on the volume of transactions, payment method, equipment costs, fraud risk, and more. By doing your research and finding the right provider, you can ensure that you're getting the best value for your money and providing your customers with a seamless payment experience

It's not uncommon to receive offers from your bank and sales representatives claiming to offer the best deal. But let's be real, it's all just a game of salesmanship and smoke and mirrors. Don't be fooled by their fancy talk and low rates, because behind the scenes there may be hidden fees waiting to pounce like a hungry lion. Monthly minimums, equipment rental fees, and lengthy contracts could be lurking in the shadows ready to ambush you. So, beware and always read the fine print, or you might find yourself singing the blues.

 **Spicy Tip:** If you are working with a one-on-one sales representative: Request a sample statement, this statement can reveal any hidden fees charged by the merchant.

When it comes to choosing the right credit card processor for your business, the options are plentiful. The key is to find the one that fits your unique business needs like a glove. If you're a wanderlust contractor who needs to take payments on the road, a phone-friendly reader might be your top priority. Or maybe you're selling a sizzling hot membership or subscription program that requires recurring charges, in which case your options will boil down to just a select few. Some platforms even have built-in customer management systems that let you keep tabs on your customers, which could come in handy.

Some popular mobile credit card processors include Square, PayPal, SumUp, Stripe, and Intuit QuickBooks GoPayment. These processors offer card readers that connect to your phone or tablet, making it easy to accept payments on the go. Additionally, they offer other payment processing options, such as invoicing and e-commerce solutions. Shop around and find the perfect fit for your business!

Chapter 20

STREAMLINING YOUR FINANCES

Small business owners have a lot on their plates. That's why it can be a little scary to realize that bookkeeping is yet another task you have to complete to keep your business running. Bookkeeping can seem like just another chore, and you might be tempted to hand it over to an accountant and forget about it. But here's the thing - as a business owner, it's important to have a basic understanding of your bookkeeping. Why, you ask? Picture this - you're driving a car with no speedometer, no fuel gauge, and no map. Sounds scary, right? It's the same with your business - if you don't understand your bookkeeping, it's like you're driving blind.

There are so many user-friendly bookkeeping programs out there that make it easy for you to keep track of your finances. When you have a clear understanding of your finances, you can make informed decisions to grow your business and keep more of your hard-earned money where it belongs - in your pocket!"

Think of bookkeeping like a financial GPS for your business. It helps you map out where you've been, where you're going, and how you're going to get there. Your bookkeeping software will help you organize, store, and analyze all your financial information in one place, making it easy to keep an eye on the financial health of your business. But that's not all - bookkeeping is also a must-do for the IRS. Yup, they require you to keep track of your income and expenses and maintain certain records.

RECORDS REQUIRED BY THE IRS
• Receipts
• Purchases
• Expenses
• Assets
• Taxes

If you neglect your bookkeeping, you might find yourself facing penalties and fines for inaccurate reporting or failure to file. Don't let that happen to you!

Decision making as a business owner can feel like a never-ending game of 'choose your own adventure', but with a good bookkeeping program by your side, you will be ready to tackle it all with confidence! Not only does bookkeeping keep the IRS happy, but it also gives you a clear understanding of your business's financial situation. With this knowledge, you can make informed decisions on big-ticket items like applying for loans, submitting grant applications, and even hiring employees.

By using your organized financial information, you can peer into the future and determine if your business can afford to take on new projects or employees. No more guesswork, just solid decisions backed by concrete data. Your financial records will help you make those big business decisions with confidence.

Spicy Tip: Test drive a few bookkeeping options. You want something you feel comfortable with, and most bookkeeping softwares offer free trial periods or affordable prices. The accounting world is full of options like FreshBooks, Quick-Books , Zoho Books, Xero, and more. While QuickBooks and FreshBooks are my personal faves, it's all about finding what works best for YOU and your business. So take your time and choose wisely!

With just a few clicks, you'll have all the insights you need to make informed decisions for your business. No more hours spent rummaging through stacks of receipts, trying to piece together how much you spent on office supplies last year. With the ability to break down your financial information in ways that make sense for you and your unique operation.

Maximizing the utility of your bookkeeping software starts with customizing its categories to align with your unique business needs. By taking the time to carefully consider the information that is most important to you, you can ensure that your expenses are effectively categorized in a way that makes sense and provides valuable insights. Remember, every business is different and deserves a tailored approach to bookkeeping.

While the IRS primarily focuses on your income and expenses, the level of detail you include in categorizing them can greatly benefit you in the long run. By breaking down your financial information into specific, meaningful categories, you gain valuable insights into your business operations and financial health.

With your bookkeeping software, you'll have access to a wealth of financial reports to help you stay on top of your business's financial performance. For instance, the profit and loss report is a must-have if you're seeking a loan from financial institutions as it provides a clear overview of your business's expenses, income, and overall financial health. The balance sheet and cash flow statement are other essential reports that give you a snapshot of your assets, liabilities, and equity, as well as an insight into your business's cash inflow and outflow. But that's not all, you can also create custom reports tailored to your specific business needs to help you make informed decisions and drive growth and success. With these reporting tools at your disposal, you're sure to be on top of your bookkeeping game.

The world of financial reporting may seem daunting with its unfamiliar terms, but there's no need to be intimidated. It's simply a matter of getting familiar with the terminology. With a little knowledge and the right tools, it can become a breeze. By selecting a bookkeeping software, you can streamline the process of tracking your expenses, automating the categorization of transactions and simplifying the overall process. Before long, you'll be able to generate clear and informative reports that provide valuable insights into your finances. So, take a deep breath, and let the power of technology work wonders for you!

Chapter 21

BRICK AND MORTAR

So you're ready to take your business to the next level and find the perfect location to bring your entrepreneurial dreams to life? Awesome! Choosing a location is like picking out the perfect out-fit - it needs to fit just right and make you feel confident and fabulous.

Here are some tips to help you find that perfect location that's just right for you and your business.

First, think about what you want your business to accomplish. Are you looking to attract foot traffic and make a splash in a bustling city center, or do you need a quieter location that's more conducive to productivity? Once you've identified your goals, you can start to think about factors like foot traffic, parking, and accessibility.

Consider your target audience - who are they and where are they located? You want to make sure that your location is convenient and accessible for your target market. Think about what other businesses and amenities are nearby - would they complement your business or compete with it?

Don't forget about the power of first impressions - make sure your location sends the right message about your brand and the quality of your products or services. Is the area clean and well-maintained? Does it reflect the image you want to project to your customers?

Employees: In addition to considering your customers, it's also important to think about your future employees when choosing a location for your business. Large corporations often choose to locate in big cities because they need access to a large pool of workers. If you have a business that doesn't rely heavily on customer traffic, such as a warehouse or shop, you may be tempted to choose a location outside the city where the cost of space is lower. However, keep in mind that commuting can be costly and time-consuming for your employees. If your location is too far from potential employees, you may have a difficult time finding and retaining talented workers. So, when selecting a location for your business, it's important to consider both the cost of the space and the availability of a skilled workforce in the area.

Zoning: Zoning regulations will play a big role in that decision. Zoning laws determine how land in a certain area can be used, which affects everything from whether you can have a storefront or a manufacturing plant, to what kind of signage you can put up. Ignoring zoning regulations can lead to costly fines and legal issues, so it's important to understand your city's rules before selecting a location. Don't know where to start? Reach out to your local government for guidance. The most common zoning types include commercial for retail spaces, industrial for manufacturing or distribution centers, and residential for living areas. Be sure to do your research and find a location that aligns with your business needs and zoning regulations to avoid any potential headaches down the road.

Ordinances: There are also certain restrictions on businesses based on their proximity to other establishments. These regulations aim to maintain a safe and harmonious community. For instance, you can't build a liquor store next to a school or place a fireworks shop in the middle of a residential neighborhood. It's important to research and understand these restrictions, also known as zoning ordinances, before choosing a location for your business. These ordinances help ensure that businesses are located in appropriate areas and don't disrupt the surrounding community.

Safety: Making sure your business location is safe for both your own well-being and the protection of your inventory. Take some time to research the crime rate in the area and visit the location at night to see if it feels secure. Pay attention to the parking lot - is it well-lit and monitored? You'll want to make sure your employees and customers feel safe coming and going, especially if you're open late. Additionally, consider if the location is prone to theft or break-ins. Don't forget to factor in security measures such as surveillance cameras, alarms, and security personnel when making your decision.

And last but not least, trust your gut! Your intuition can be a powerful tool when it comes to finding the perfect location for your business. Visit different locations, talk to other business owners in the area, and imagine your business operating in each space. If a location feels right, go for it!

Remember, finding the perfect location for your business is like finding the perfect partner - it takes time, effort, and a little bit of luck. But with these tips in mind, you'll be well on your way to finding a location that's the perfect match for your business.

Chapter 22

UNDERSTANDING COMMERCIAL LEASES

Commercial leases are a whole different ball game compared to those boring old residential leases. There's no one-size-fits-all approach here, as every business has its own unique needs and requirements. From storefronts to warehouses to regular office spaces, the possibilities are truly endless!

Don't fret. Whether you're on the hunt for a small office or a massive warehouse, there's a lease out there that's just perfect for you. Keep in mind, however, that there are several types of commercial leases, each with its own unique terms and conditions.

Each type of lease has its own set of pros and cons, but with a little searching, you'll find the perfect spot for your business! Unlike the competitive nature of residential leases, commercial spaces are in abundance, especially in the post-COVID era. Don't be afraid to negotiate with your landlord and find the right lease that works for your business.

There are many factors you can negotiate in a lease agreement, such as the length of the lease, the amount of the security deposit, and the rate at which the rent increases over time. You may even be able to negotiate some of the costs associated with building out the space or obtaining a certificate of occupancy. Don't be afraid to ask for what you want, as the worst that can happen is that the landlord says no. Remember, negotiations are a two-way street, so be prepared to compromise as well. A successful negotiation can result in a lease agreement that benefits both you and your landlord.

TYPES OF COMMERCIAL LEASES

1. **Gross lease:** This all-inclusive lease provides a predictable rent payment for tenants, as the landlord is responsible for paying all operating expenses. No unexpected costs here, which can be a huge relief for small businesses and startups. Just keep in mind that the fixed rent amount may be higher than a net lease, as the landlord is assuming all operating expenses.

2. **Net lease:** In this type of lease, the tenant pays a lower base rent and is responsible for some or all of the property's operating expenses. There are three types of net leases:

   - **Single Net Lease (SN)**: tenant pays base rent and some property taxes, landlord pays remaining taxes, insurance, and maintenance costs.
   - **Double Net Lease (DN)**: tenant pays base rent, some property taxes, and insurance, landlord pays remaining taxes and maintenance costs.
   - **Triple Net Lease (NNN)**: tenant pays base rent, all property taxes, insurance, and maintenance costs, landlord pays none of these expenses.

3. **Modified Gross lease:** A combination of a gross and net lease, a modified gross lease allows for a more even distribution of operating expenses between landlord and tenant. The base rent includes some of the operating expenses, while the landlord is responsible for others.

4. **Percentage lease:** Common in retail settings, this type of lease allows the landlord to benefit from the tenant's success by collecting a percentage of their sales revenue, in addition to a lower base rent amount. However, tenants may be required to share a portion of their revenue with the landlord, which can be risky.

5. **Ground lease:** This lease allows tenants to lease land from a landlord and construct and maintain their own building on the property. This can be beneficial for businesses that want to preserve capital or do not have the financing to purchase property.

6. **Sublease:** This allows tenants to sublet all or a portion of their leased space to another tenant, which can be useful for reducing rental costs or providing temporary space.

7. **Build-to-Suit lease:** This type of lease allows the tenant to have a space customized to their specific needs, with the landlord agreeing to build a space to the tenant's specifications. The tenant usually agrees to lease the space for a long-term period, typically 10-20 years.

Each type of lease has its own set of pros and cons, but with a little searching, you'll find the perfect spot for your business! Unlike the competitive nature of residential leases, commercial spaces are in abundance, especially in the post-COVID era. Don't be afraid to negotiate with your landlord and find the right lease that works for your business.

There are many factors you can negotiate in a lease agreement, such as the length of the lease, the amount of the security deposit, and the rate at which the rent increases over time. You may even be able to negotiate some of the costs associated with building out the space or obtaining a certificate of occupancy. Don't be afraid to ask for what you want, as the worst that can happen is that the landlord says no. Remember, negotiations are a two-way street, so be prepared to compromise as well. A successful negotiation can result in a lease agreement that benefits both you and your landlord.

Chapter 23

CERTIFICATE OF OCCUPANCY

Congratulations on finding the perfect space for your business! But before you can officially open your doors to the public, there is one important hurdle you'll need to clear: obtaining a Certificate of Occupancy (CO). This certificate is a legal document that indicates that the building meets all necessary safety and health codes and is suitable for occupancy.

To ensure that you are on the right track to getting a CO, it's important to remember that each city has its own unique process. Make sure to do your research and find out what the requirements are for your specific location. It's also worth noting that if your business is located in an unincorporated area, the process may be different or you may not even need a CO.

Step 1: Check with Your Local Government

The first step is to do your research and check with your local government to find out what specific requirements and regulations apply to your business. Different types of businesses may have different requirements, and different jurisdictions may have different rules.

To make things easier, start by visiting your local government's website or building department. They should be able to provide you with a list of the documents and permits that you will need to apply for a CO. You can also check to see if they have a liaison or dedicated team member to assist new business owners with the process.

Step 2: Prepare the Necessary Documentation

Once you have a list of requirements, you can begin gathering the necessary documentation. This may include architectural plans, blueprints, plumbing diagrams, electrical layouts, fire safety plans, and more. You may also need to provide proof of insurance, business licenses, and tax identification numbers. This will depend on your city.

Step 3: Schedule Inspections

Once you have the necessary documentation, the next step is to schedule inspections to ensure that your building meets all necessary safety and health codes. Inspections will vary depending on the jurisdiction, but common inspections include structural, electrical, plumbing, mechanical and fire safety inspections. It's important to note that inspections may need to be scheduled in a specific order, so be sure to follow the guidelines provided by your local government.

Dealing with inspectors can be a mixed bag. Some are friendly, helpful, and a pleasure to work with, while others can be a bit difficult to handle. Regardless of their personality, it's important to treat all inspectors with respect and professionalism. By maintaining a friendly attitude and being cooperative, you can help ensure a smoother and more positive experience during the inspection process. Remember, a little kindness can go a long way!

Step 4: Address Any Issues

If any issues are found during inspections, you'll need to address them before you can obtain your CO. Depending on the severity of the issue, this may involve hiring a professional to make repairs, making changes to your building plans, or obtaining additional permits.

Step 5: Obtain Your Certificate of Occupancy

Once all inspections are complete and any issues have been addressed, you'll need to submit your application for a CO. If everything is in order, your local government will issue your CO, and you'll be free to open your doors to the public! It's an exciting moment and a big milestone for any business owner, so celebrate accordingly. Congratulations, and here's to a successful future!

Chapter 24

RISKY BUSINESS

R unning a business is a risky business! But with the right insurance coverage, you can protect yourself from potential losses and liabilities. Sure, insurance can be a little pricey at times, but it's worth it in the long run. Not only does it protect you and your business, but it can also help you attract more customers and opportunities. Just like how you wouldn't buy a car without insurance, you shouldn't run a business without it either.

As your business grows and you start working with other businesses or clients, you'll quickly realize that having insurance is often a requirement. It's not just for your own peace of mind, but also for the peace of mind of your clients and partners.

So, what are the different types of business insurance? Well, there are many! Some of the most common types of business insurance include general liability insurance, property insurance, professional liability insurance, and workers' compensation insurance. Each type of insurance provides coverage for different types of risks and liabilities, so it's important to understand what you need for your specific business.

For example, if you have a physical storefront or office, property insurance can protect you from damage or loss of property due to theft, fire, or other unforeseen events. If you provide professional services, such as consulting or legal services, professional liability insurance can protect you from potential lawsuits or claims of negligence.

If you have employees, you'll also need workers' compensation insurance to cover injuries or illnesses that occur on the job. Professional liability insurance, also known as errors and omissions insurance, can protect your business in case of negligence or mistakes made by you or your employees.

Other types of business insurance include business interruption insurance, which can provide coverage if your business is unable to operate due to a covered event, such as a natural disaster or equipment breakdown. Cyber liability insurance can protect your business from data breaches or other cyber threats. Finally, commercial auto insurance is necessary if your business uses vehicles for business purposes.

The key is to assess the specific risks that your business may face and choose the insurance coverage that fits your needs. Don't wait until it's too late – insurance may not be the most exciting topic, but it's part of running a successful business. It may be a pain in the wallet at first, but it's a small price to pay for the peace of mind and protection it provides.

Chapter 25

LIKE A BOSS

Think back to the best teacher you've ever had. What made them so great? Was it simply because their class was easy? Probably not. The best teachers are often the ones who serve as great leaders. They inspire, motivate, and believe in their students. They challenge their students to be their best selves, and they foster a sense of trust and respect in the classroom.

The same principles that make a great teacher also apply to leadership in the business world. As a leader, your role is not just to manage your team, but to inspire and motivate them to do their best work. You need to create an environment where your team members feel valued, supported, and empowered to take ownership of their work.

Leading isn't about being the bossy boots who tells everyone what to do. That's a one-way ticket to becoming the office outcast! As a business owner, you've got to step up your game and become a leader.

Leadership can be both a fulfilling and daunting task, and it's important to regularly assess and improve your skills. One easy way to do this is to reflect on your experiences in your personal life. Do your friends and family members seek your advice or support? How do you handle communication during challenging conversations? These skills can translate into your role as a leader in the workplace and help you to create a positive and productive work environment.

Even if you already consider yourself to be a master communicator or leader, there is always room for improvement. Leadership is a continuous journey that requires lifelong learning and growth. By actively seeking out opportunities to improve your skills, such as attending workshops or seeking feedback from your team, you can continue to develop your leadership abilities and create a more successful business.

By honing your communication and leadership skills, you can help to create a culture of trust, collaboration, and innovation in your workplace. An effective leader is an excellent communicator who can use psychology and NLP (Neuro-Linguistic Programming) to influence and motivate their team. You don't need to be a Jedi mind master to get results! It's about understanding how people think and behave, and using that knowledge to create a positive and productive work environment.

Using positive reinforcement can be a powerful motivator. Recognize and reward your team members for their hard work, and create a culture where people feel valued and appreciated. Understanding the "love languages" of your team can also help - some people respond best to praise, while others may prefer tangible rewards like a promotion or bonus.

If you haven't read *The 5 Love Languages* by Gary Chapman yet, I highly recommend it! This book provides a framework for understanding how people express and receive love and appreciation, which can be useful in both personal and professional relationships. By understanding the different ways that people prefer to give and receive recognition and appreciation, you can tailor your communication and leadership style to better suit the needs of your team. So, whether you're trying to improve your personal relationships or your professional ones, this book is definitely worth checking out!

In addition to positive reinforcement, there are many other ways to use psychology to lead effectively. For example, you can create a culture of trust and respect by being transparent and honest with your team, and by actively listening to their concerns and feedback. This creates a sense of purpose and autonomy among your team members. People are more motivated when they feel like they have control over their work and are working towards a meaningful goal. So, work with your team to set clear and meaningful goals, and empower them to take ownership of their work.

Being an effective leader requires effort and commitment. However, it's also important to recognize that not everyone is cut out for leadership, and that's okay. If you're struggling with communication or finding it difficult to lead your team, it's important to seek out the resources and support you need to be successful.

One option is to leverage the expertise of an HR department, which can provide guidance and support on issues related to communication, team building, and leadership. If your business isn't quite ready for an HR department, consider reaching out to external resources, such as coaches or mentors, to help you develop your leadership skills.

Another option is to evaluate the rest of your team to see if there is someone who is a natural leader. Look for individuals who others naturally look up to and follow, and consider giving them additional responsibility or even promoting them to a managerial position. This can not only provide a more effective leader for your team but also allow you to focus on areas where you excel.

Remember, being a leader isn't just about being in charge. It's about inspiring and motivating your team to work towards a common goal. By being open to feedback, seeking out support and resources, and recognizing the strengths of your team, you can develop your leadership skills and create a positive and successful work environment.

The Bad Apple

Dealing with frustrating employees can be a major headache for employers. However, it's important to remember that just like in personal relationships, it takes two to tango. While it's true that you can't control every situation or individual, it's important to take a proactive approach to addressing problematic behavior.

Sometimes, despite your best efforts to hire the right people and create an awesome work culture, there will still be employees who cause issues in the workplace. This can be due to personal problems or simply a poor fit for the job. It's important to recognize when these issues are impacting the team and take action to address them.

But how can you do this effectively? It starts with communication and empathy. By taking the time to understand the root of the problem and approaching the situation with a compassionate attitude, you can work towards a solution that benefits both the individual and the business.

Of course, this isn't always an easy task. It can be challenging to balance the needs of the individual with the needs of the team and the business as a whole. That's why it's important to have clear boundaries and expectations in place, as well as a willingness to take appropriate action when necessary.

At the end of the day, managing employees is all about finding the right balance. By taking a proactive, empathetic approach and being willing to make tough decisions when needed, you can create a positive and productive work environment for your team.

Being an effective manager requires a range of skills and strategies to ensure the success of your team.

TIPS FOR MANAGING EMPLOYEES

1. **Open Communication:** Have a one-on-one conversation with the employee and clearly outline the issue or behavior that needs to be addressed. Listen to their perspective and offer constructive feedback on how they can improve.

2. **Set Clear Expectations:** Make sure that the employee understands what is expected of them, and what the consequences will be if they do not meet those expectations.

3. **Offer Support:** Provide the employee with resources, training, or coaching to help them improve. This shows that you are invested in their success and can help to build a positive working relationship.

4. **Document Incidents**: Keep a record of any incidents or issues that arise, including dates, times, and specific details. This documentation can be used to track progress or as evidence if further action is required.

5. **Follow Company Policies:** Ensure that any actions taken are in line with company policies and procedures. This helps to maintain fairness and consistency in the workplace.

6. **Seek Assistance:** If the issue persists, consider involving human resources or seeking professional advice from a management consultant or coach. They can provide guidance and support to help you manage the situation effectively.

7. **Build a Positive Relationship:** Take the time to get to know your employees, their strengths, weaknesses, and goals. This will help you build trust and rapport, leading to a more productive and positive work environment.

8. **Communicate Effectively:** Clear communication is key to avoiding misunderstandings and conflicts in the workplace. Make sure you are delivering your message clearly and concisely, and encourage employees to express their thoughts and concerns.

9. **Provide Feedback:** Regular feedback is crucial to employee growth and development. Offer constructive criticism and praise where necessary, and be sure to highlight specific areas for improvement.

10. **Empower Your Team:** Give your employees the freedom to make decisions and take ownership of their work. This will help build their confidence and improve their performance.

11. **Recognize Achievements:** Acknowledge the hard work and achievements of your employees, whether it be a simple thank you or a formal recognition program. This will boost morale and motivate your team to continue performing at their best.

12. **Changing Employee Roles:** Consider re-evaluating the skills and interests of your employees and determine if they are better suited for a different job in the company. This can help to improve job satisfaction and performance, leading to a more productive and engaged workforce.

Remember that employees are the backbone of any organization, and investing in their well-being and development can help foster a positive work environment. However, there may be instances where an employee is not meeting expectations despite your best efforts to support and guide them. In such cases, it's important to approach the situation with care and respect.

Documentation is crucial in any employee-related issue, and this is especially true when it comes to termination. Ensure that you have a clear record of any incidents or issues that have led to the decision to let the employee go. It's also important to be familiar with relevant laws and regulations in your state to ensure that the process is handled professionally and ethically.

Approaching employee termination with professionalism and care not only helps to mitigate potential legal issues, but it also demonstrates that you value and respect your employees. By providing support, guidance, and feedback throughout the process, you can help to ensure a smooth transition for both the employee and the rest of the team.

Chapter 26

EMPLOYEE MAGNET

Hiring and retaining top talent is like finding a four-leaf clover in a field of grass. It's rare and takes some luck, but don't fret, there's a secret to keeping your dream team together - creating a fantastic culture. Think of it like a magnet that draws in the best people and keeps them coming back for more. You want a culture that makes employees feel like they're part of a family, appreciated, and constantly growing in their careers. It's like Hogwarts, but for the workplace - where magic and progress happen every day!

The key to building this mystical culture is authenticity. Employees want to work for a company that truly lives and breathes its values. They want a company that treats its employees just as well as its customers. That's why it's important for leaders to lead by example and embody the company's core beliefs. It's not always easy, but it's important to keep it real and avoid office politics, egos, and internal competition that can get in the way of authenticity.

Now, let's talk about moving people around. Sometimes employees start off in one job, but find they're better suited for another role. And that's okay! It's important to recognize when someone isn't happy in their current position and find a better fit for them. It's like playing musical chairs - but with jobs! By doing this, you'll keep your employees happy and engaged, and they'll be more likely to stick around for the long haul.

But how do you keep your employees really, truly happy? You gotta speak their love language, my friend! Everyone has a different way they like to be appreciated and motivated. For some, it's words of affirmation, for others it's quality time, acts of service, gifts, or a simple high-five. By learning what your employees respond to, you can keep them feeling loved and valued. And a happy employee is a productive employee, right?

Nobody is going to work as hard as you or care as much as you about your business. But given the right environment, employees will care a lot about their work because they feel a deep connection with the company, its leaders, and their team. And it all starts from the moment you begin the hiring process. When you're crafting your job description, think not only about what you want from the employee, but also what the employee can expect from the job. Be honest and transparent - it's the best way to attract the right people to your team.

Hiring Platforms: When it comes to hiring people, there's no shortage of options out there. The key is to find the best fit for your business and the type of talent you're seeking. Keep in mind that different platforms cater to different types of job seekers. For instance, if you're looking for a professional with a specific skill set, you may want to place your ads on sites like LinkedIn, Indeed or Monster. These platforms are designed to connect businesses with experienced and highly-skilled professionals.

On the other hand, if you're hiring for a general labor job or a part-time position, social media platforms like Facebook or Instagram may be a good option. You can post job listings on your company

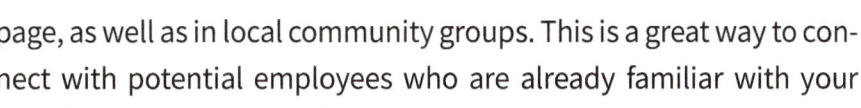

page, as well as in local community groups. This is a great way to connect with potential employees who are already familiar with your brand and may be more likely to be a good cultural fit.

Another option to consider is using a recruiting agency. These agencies have extensive networks and can help you find highly qualified candidates for specialized roles. They also take care of the initial screening process, which can save you a lot of time and effort.

If you're looking to attract younger talent, you may want to consider using campus job boards or attending job fairs at local colleges and universities. This is a great way to connect with students and recent graduates who are looking to launch their careers.

And don't forget about word-of-mouth referrals. Your current employees can be a great source of talent, and they may know someone who would be a great fit for your business. Encourage your employees to spread the word about any job openings!

Interviewing: Interviewing is a skill that requires practice and experience. Simply attending a few interviews or conducting a handful of them yourself doesn't make you an expert. In fact, being good at interviews involves much more than just being a smooth talker. It's about understanding human behavior, communication, and psychology.

When you're conducting an interview, it's important to think of it like a fishing expedition. You can't just cast your line and hope for the best – you need to know what kind of bait to use and how to reel in your catch. Similarly, you need to know how to ask the right questions and create an environment that encourages the interviewee to open up and share their thoughts and experiences.

But interviewing isn't just about asking questions; it's about actively listening to what the interviewee has to say. That means paying attention to their tone of voice, body language, and the nuances in their responses. It takes practice and skill to know when to dig deeper and ask follow-up questions, or when to pivot and steer the conversation in a different direction.

As you conduct interviews, it's important to remember that the real value often comes from what the interviewee says, not just from the questions you ask. That's why it's important to create a comfortable environment that encourages the interviewee to open up and share their thoughts and experiences.

But why is it so important to be a good interviewer? Well, hiring the wrong person can be costly. From the cost of posting job ads, to the time spent sifting through candidates, interviewing, training, background checks and onboarding, the expenses can add up quickly. So, it's important to get it right – or at least get it right most of the time.

One way to improve your interviewing skills and increase your chances of hiring the right person is to consider working interviews. This allows your prospective hire to get a feel for your company and culture, and it allows you to get to know your candidate and see how they mesh with the rest of the team. With a little bit of practice and patience, you'll be reeling in top talent in no time.

So whether you're exploring hiring platforms, perfecting your interviewing skills, or creating a magical workplace culture, remember that finding and retaining the best talent takes effort, but it's definitely not impossible. With the right strategies and a little bit of luck (or a four-leaf clover), you can build a dream team that will take your business to new heights.

Chapter 27

CONTRACTOR VS EMPLOYEE

If you're looking to hire someone, you might be tempted to classify them as a contractor instead of an employee. After all, that means you can avoid paying those pesky payroll taxes, and you're off the hook for providing benefits like unemployment. But hold on just a minute. Misclassifying your workers can lead to some serious trouble, and maybe you're just not sure of the difference. Let's clear things up.

In simple terms, a contractor is someone you hire to do a specific job or project for a set amount of money. Contractors are generally considered self-employed and are responsible for paying their own taxes, insurance, and other expenses. They usually work on a temporary basis and may work for multiple clients at the same time.

On the other hand, an employee is someone you hire to work for your business on a regular basis. You as the employer are responsible for paying payroll taxes, providing benefits, and complying with employment laws. Employees typically work for a set number of hours per week or month and may have a set schedule or work location.

It's important to properly classify workers as either contractors or employees, as misclassification can lead to legal and financial consequences. The key factors that determine whether someone is a contractor or an employee include the level of control the employer has over the worker, the degree of independence the worker has, and the nature of the work being performed.

EMPLOYEES VS CONTRACT LABOR

- A freelance graphic designer who is hired on a project-by-project basis is generally considered a contractor.
- An administrative assistant who works in an office full-time and is paid a salary is generally considered an employee.
- A construction worker who is hired to work on a specific building project for a set period of time is generally considered a contractor.
- A retail store clerk who is scheduled to work specific hours and receives hourly pay is generally considered an employee.
- An independent consultant who provides services to multiple clients and sets their own hours and fees is generally considered a contractor.
- An IT specialist who works full-time for a company and receives a regular salary is generally considered an employee.

A big clue is how your employee contractor gets paid, here is some information directly from the IRS website:

Employee: An employee pay period must remain the same unless formally changed. Pay periods vary from one week to one month. Federal and state laws require that an employee be paid on the normal pay date or earlier if the paycheck is not negotiable on the normal pay date, which can occur on holidays.

- Earns either an hourly rate or a salary
- Your employee will receive a W-2 at the end of the year.

Contractor: Accounts Payable pays a contractor after receiving an invoice. The terms of the contract or Statement of Work dictate when payments are made, such as upon completion of a task or by periodic amounts. Contractors are not paid by payroll staff in most businesses.

- A contract may be for a total amount. It could be for an hourly, daily, or weekly amount that ends on a specific date or a total amount to be paid when the job is completed.
- It's important to note that according to IRS regulations, businesses are required to file a 1099-MISC form for all non-employee service providers who were paid $600 or more in a given tax year. This includes independent contractors, freelancers, and other self-employed individuals who provided services to the business.

If you are unsure, just give the Department of Labor a call - they're actually pretty nice and always happy to chat.

Chapter 28

NLP AND PSYCHOLOGY

H ere's a secret: if you want to succeed in business, you need to understand what makes people tick and how to meet their needs. Business is all about people! It's not just about crunching numbers and reading graphs; it's about understanding human behavior.

To succeed in business, it definitely helps to be a people person. However, not everyone is naturally skilled at it, and that's okay! You can still learn how to read people, communicate effectively, and build strong relationships with customers and team members. While some people may have a natural talent for it, others can develop these skills through practice and experience. Don't be afraid to step out of your comfort zone and learn how to win hearts and minds. It's what sets successful businesses apart from the rest.

Empathy, emotional intelligence, and conflict resolution are pillars of success for any business owner. They'll help you navigate challenging situations with ease and cultivate stronger, more meaningful connections with the people you work with. I know you can't become a psychology expert overnight, but that doesn't mean you can't start now!

Here are some fun things you can start practicing. But remember psychology and persuasion should be about building trust and creating win-win outcomes, not manipulation. Good luck!

NLP mirroring: NLP mirroring is a technique used in Neuro-Linguistic Programming (NLP) which was invented by Richard Bandler and John Grinder in the 1970s. NLP is a technique used to build rapport with another person by mirroring or matching their physical movements, tone of voice, and language.

The idea behind mirroring is that people tend to like and trust others who are similar to them. By matching another person's body language, tone of voice, and choice of words, you can create a sense of familiarity and connection. This can be especially useful in business settings, such as when you're meeting a potential client or trying to persuade someone to see things from your perspective. Next time you're at lunch with a friend try it out.

NLP IN ACTION

- **Body language**: If the person you're talking to leans forward, you can lean forward too. If they cross their arms, you can do the same. This creates a sense of similarity and helps build rapport.
- **Tone of voice**: If the person you're talking to speaks quickly, you can speed up your own speech. If they have a soft, gentle tone, you can adjust your own tone to match. This can help you build a sense of harmony with the other person.
- **Language:** If the person you're talking to uses specific words or phrases, you can incorporate them into your own language. This creates a sense of familiarity and shows that you understand their perspective.

It's important to note that mirroring should never be used as a manipulative "magic trick" to trick or deceive people. Instead, it should be used as a way to create genuine connection and make people feel comfortable around you. If you observe couples and friends in public, you may notice that they often mirror each other's behaviors, which can help to strengthen their bond.

If you're interested in using mirroring to build rapport with others, it's important to approach it with a spirit of authenticity and respect. With practice, you can develop the skills to use mirroring in a way that feels natural and creates a sense of connection with those around you.

The words you use:

The words you use can have a huge impact on your mindset and the way you approach challenges. For example, instead of using the word "problem," which can have negative connotations, try using the word "challenge" instead.

When you view obstacles as challenges, you're more likely to see them as opportunities for growth and improvement. You can approach them with a positive attitude and a willingness to learn and adapt.

That's not the only word that can have a big impact on your mindset. Another word to watch out for is "but." It might seem harmless enough, yet it can actually undermine the positive message that came before it.

For example, if you say "You did a great job, but..." the person you're talking to is likely to focus on the negative part of the sentence and feel discouraged. However, if you say "You did a great job, and..." the person is more likely to feel positive and motivated to keep up the good work.

Here is another, replace the word "if" with "when" in your vocabulary. By doing so, you are affirming your belief that you will achieve your goals and overcome obstacles, rather than simply entertaining the possibility of success.

It's amazing how much difference a small change in wording can make. By being mindful of the words you use, you can create a more positive and supportive environment, both for yourself and for those around you. So, next time you're speaking with someone, try swapping out negative words for more positive ones and see how it affects the conversation.

How to Win Friends and Influence People by Dale Carnegie is an exceptional book that can help you learn more about effective communication. It highlights the importance of not only what you say, but how you say it. Whether you're in sales, leadership, or even when asking for funding from a banker, the ability to communicate your message clearly can be incredibly beneficial. Not only can this help you achieve your professional goals, but it can also have a positive impact on your personal relationships.

The book offers practical tips on how to become a more effective communicator, such as active listening, showing genuine interest in others, and offering sincere praise. These principles can be applied in a variety of situations, from one-on-one conversations to public speaking.

Bottom line, effective communication is a crucial skill to have, whether you're a business owner or just going through life. It involves various components such as, maintaining eye contact, using positive body language, and choosing the right words.

At some point in our lives, we all have to have difficult conversations, encourage people who are going through personal challenges, or simply interact with others on a daily basis. Developing effective communication skills takes practice, but it's worth the effort.

Improving your communication abilities is an integral part of advancing both personally and professionally. It can help you present your ideas more persuasively, negotiate more effectively, and build trust with your colleagues and customers.

Remember, communication skills are not innate abilities, but skills that can be developed and refined with practice. By investing in improving your communication skills, you can experience better outcomes both personally and professionally.

The good news is that there are resources available to help improve your communication skills. Books, courses, and coaching are all great ways to get started. Ultimately, the key is to practice consistently and seek feedback so you can continue to improve.

Start having conversations with your friends, family, and even strangers. Try out some of the tips you've learned and see how they work in real life. By applying what you've learned, you'll start developing a better understanding of human behavior.

Chapter 29

AUTOMATE TO INNOVATE

A utomation has come a long way in recent years, and it's not just for big corporations anymore. Small businesses and startups can also benefit from automation tools to streamline their workflows and increase productivity. By using technology to automate tasks such as data entry, report generation, and email marketing, you can free up time for more strategic and creative work.

One of the best things about automation is that it can make work more fun. When you're not bogged down with tedious tasks, you can spend more time on the things you're passionate about.

AUTOMATING YOUR BUSINESS

1. **Automate Data Entry and Processing:** Manual data entry is a snooze-fest prone to errors. Use automated systems like CRM software, accounting software, or inventory management systems to speed up the process and improve accuracy.
2. **Automate Communication and Collaboration:** Ditch the endless email chains and try collaboration tools like instant messaging, video conferencing, and project management software to improve teamwork and work more efficiently.

4. **Automate Marketing and Sales:** Automate lead generation, email campaigns, and social media management using tools like Salesforce, Hubspot, and Keap. Let the bots do the grunt work while you brainstorm creative marketing ideas.

5. **Automate Customer Service:** Meet customer expectations for fast and efficient service with a mix of chatbots, online contact forms, and customer portals.

6. **Automate HR Tasks:** Use services like QuickBooks and Gusto to automate HR tasks like onboarding, benefits administration, and payroll. No more paper checks!

7. **Automate Billing:** Use invoicing tools like FreshBooks and QuickBooks to automate invoicing and get paid faster.

8. **Automate Paperwork:** Use form programs like JotForm, DocuSign, and Formstack to capture all necessary data and signatures digitally.

But before you get too excited and start automating everything in sight, let's remember that automation is not a silver bullet solution. Each business is unique and requires a tailored approach to automation. Don't be afraid to mix and match different programs to find the right fit for your specific needs. You'll still need to use your judgment and creativity to decide when and where automation makes sense.

While automation can help increase productivity and efficiency, it's important to maintain a human touch and not rely solely on technology. At the end of the day, business is about people and relationships. So don't forget to foster personal connections and provide excellent customer service that goes beyond just automation. Remember, a smile and a friendly voice can go a long way in creating happy and loyal customers.

Chapter 30

THE POWER OF LETTING GO

Owning a business is like wearing a lot of different hats - some of them might not be your style, but you gotta rock them anyway. And if you stumble across a task that's completely out of your comfort zone, don't panic! You'll figure it out. It's all part of the process. You will learn to embrace the challenges and find joy in the responsibilities that come naturally to you. Who knows, you might just surprise yourself!

If you have a business partner, you can divide the responsibilities based on your strengths and weaknesses. This will give you both the chance to showcase your unique talents and abilities. Whether you excel at building relationships with people, analyzing data, or unleashing your creativity, there are plenty of opportunities to shine.

Remember, nobody is perfect. It's okay to make mistakes and learn as you go. In fact, it's essential to keep growing and evolving as your business grows. As your company expands, you may find that certain parts of it outgrow your skill abilities, time, or earnings capabilities. When this happens, it's important to reassess the situation and be willing to make tough decisions. Sometimes, the best move is to hire someone who's more experienced or skilled than you to handle the task.

Delegating can be challenging, especially if you're used to being hands-on with every aspect of your business. But it's a recommended step if you want your business to succeed. When you hire someone to handle a job, it will free you up to focus on what you're best at. This can make a significant impact on your company, as you'll be able to devote more time and energy to tasks that promote growth.

Not every task that you hire out needs to be handled by an expert. In fact, some tasks don't require any particular expertise at all. This includes tasks in your home life, like cleaning your house or taking care of your yard. If these tasks are stressing you out and taking up too much of your time, hire someone to take on those responsibilities. By outsourcing these tasks, you'll free up more time and energy to focus on your work.

One of the biggest challenges of being an entrepreneur is letting go of control. However, if you're trying to run a business at full capacity, you won't be able to focus on growth and innovation. In order to succeed, you need to learn how to delegate effectively and trust others to handle important tasks.

Many business owners struggle with this, and it's a common way that business owners stunt their growth. However, it's necessary to relinquish control if you want your company to flourish. When you bring in new hires, they may not do things the exact same way you do, and that's okay. In fact, it's a good thing - it means that you're bringing in fresh perspectives and ideas that can help your business grow and evolve.

By learning to let go, you'll be able to focus on the big picture and make strategic decisions that can take your business to the next level.

You'll also be able to cultivate a strong team culture that encourages creativity, collaboration, and innovation.

Remember, letting go of control is not a sign of weakness - it's a sign of strength. It means that you're willing to trust others and work together to achieve a common goal. So if you want to see your business succeed and grow, learn to delegate effectively and embrace the power of teamwork.

START WITH THIS

1. **Make a list:** Start by making a list of all the tasks you currently do on a daily, weekly, or monthly basis. Then, highlight the ones that could be delegated to someone else. This exercise will help you identify areas where you can free up some of your time and delegate tasks to employees.

2. **Practice communication:** One of the most important aspects of delegating tasks is clear communication. To practice this skill, try giving your employees detailed instructions for completing a task that you would normally do yourself. Then, have them complete the task and provide you with feedback. This exercise will help you refine your communication skills and ensure that tasks are completed correctly.

3. **Track progress:** To ensure that tasks are being completed correctly, track your employees' progress and provide them with feedback. This will help you identify areas where your employees may need additional training or support, and will also help you build trust and confidence in your team.

Chapter 31

BLIND SPOTS

Imagine you've been working your tail off, doing everything you can to succeed, but for some reason, you keep hitting a wall. You're not sure what's going wrong, and it's driving you crazy! The thing is, you forgot to check your blind spots!

As humans, we all have blind spots. These are the things we're unaware of that can cause major roadblocks in our success. It's like driving a semi-truck without checking your mirrors – you're just asking for trouble!

For example, if you have a tendency to micromanage your team without realizing it, you could be limiting their creativity and productivity. Or if you have biases that you're not aware of, you could be making hiring or promotion decisions based on things that don't actually matter, like someone's gender or age.

The tricky thing about blind spots is that they're often caused by our own biases and beliefs. Our brains naturally filter information in a way that supports our existing opinions, which can cause us to overlook things that don't fit into our view of the world or make us uncomfortable.

For instance, let's say you hate confrontation. You might avoid difficult conversations with team members, hoping that problems will just go away on their own. But in reality, this could be a recipe for disaster, as you may not be fully aware of the issues that need to be addressed. This is just one example of how blind spots can hold us back in business and life. The key is to be aware of our own biases and actively seek out alternative perspectives to broaden our understanding.

One of the first steps in overcoming blind spots is to become aware of them. This can be achieved by seeking feedback from others, actively listening to constructive criticism, and reflecting on our own thoughts, feelings, and behaviors. Once you have identified your blind spots, you can begin to work on addressing them.

This process can involve questioning our own assumptions and biases, challenging our beliefs, and exposing ourselves to diverse perspectives and experiences. It may also involve seeking out mentors or coaches who can provide guidance and support as we work to overcome our blind spots.

Try this self-reflection exercise: Start by asking yourself questions.

1. What assumptions do I have about myself, others, or the world that might be limiting my perspective?
2. Are there any topics or situations that I tend to avoid or dismiss without considering alternative viewpoints?
3. Are there any areas in my life or business where I consistently struggle or feel stuck?

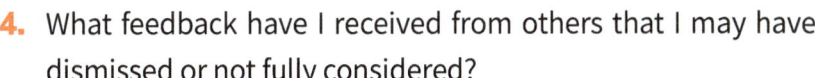

4. What feedback have I received from others that I may have dismissed or not fully considered?
5. Are there any patterns or habits that I have that might be preventing me from seeing things clearly?
6. How do my values and beliefs impact my decision-making and problem-solving processes?
7. Am I open to feedback and willing to consider different perspectives?
8. What steps can I take to challenge my assumptions and broaden my understanding of myself and the world around me?

> As you reflect on these questions, try to be honest with yourself and avoid getting defensive or dismissive of any uncomfortable truths that may arise.

Developing a habit of checking for blind spots can be a powerful tool in this process. By making a conscious effort to regularly assess our own thoughts, feelings, and behaviors, we can become more aware of our blind spots and work to overcome them. This may involve setting aside time each day or week for self-reflection and introspection, seeking out feedback from others, and actively seeking out new experiences and perspectives.

Once you become aware of your blind spots, you can work to overcome them and get back on track. But let's be real - this is no easy feat. Blind spots are like pesky little gremlins that have made a cozy home in our brains, and they don't like to leave without a fight.

Challenging our blind spots can be uncomfortable, sometimes even painful. It requires us to confront long-held beliefs, biases, and assumptions that we may not even realize we have. This process of self-reflection and growth can be difficult, but it's also incredibly rewarding.

It's like cleaning out your closet. At first, it can be overwhelming to sort through all the clutter and figure out what to keep and what to let go of. But once you start, it becomes easier to see what's important and what's just taking up space. The same goes for our blind spots - once we start to acknowledge and address them, we can start to let go of the beliefs and biases that are no longer serving us.

Another helpful tool is to practice empathy and understanding towards others. By putting yourself in someone else's shoes, you can start to recognize your own biases and assumptions. This can be particularly useful in addressing issues of diversity and inclusion in the workplace, where unconscious biases can have a significant impact on hiring and promotion decisions.

Ultimately, challenging our blind spots is about being open to growth and change. It's about acknowledging that we don't have all the answers, and that there is always room for improvement. By making a habit of checking for blind spots, we can continue to grow and evolve, both personally and professionally.

So, before you make any big decisions, take a step back and ask yourself – could I be missing something here? Am I looking at this situation with clear eyes?

By looking at the situation with fresh eyes, you give yourself the chance to gain a deeper understanding of the thought patterns and behaviors that may have been leading you astray. It's like taking a moment to clear the fog from your mind and see things more clearly. Truth is, we all need a little clarity sometimes!

Reflecting on what led you to the situation in the first place can be tough, but it's a crucial step towards making positive changes in your life. It's like being your own detective, investigating the root cause of the problem. And who knows, maybe you'll uncover something new and surprising about yourself in the process!

Now, I won't sugarcoat it - this kind of introspection can feel very unpleasant. But hey, change is never easy. Think of it like going to the gym - it may be hard work at first, but once you start seeing results, it feels so rewarding!

Once you've identified the root cause of the issue, you can start working towards a solution and make a plan to avoid repeating the same mistakes in the future. And that's the goal, right? To learn and grow from our experiences, so we can be better and stronger moving forward.

Just remember, nobody's perfect. We all make mistakes, it's just part of being human. But being aware and taking steps towards positive change is what sets us apart. So go ahead, clear those eyes, and get ready to take on whatever life throws your way!

Chapter 32

THE PAYROLL AND HR HANDBOOK

Human resources and payroll are two fundamental components of any organization. Even if you don't have dedicated personnel for these areas, you can't afford to ignore them. Not only can non-compliance result in costly legal issues, but it can also harm your reputation and negatively impact employee morale. Trust me, employees won't hesitate to speak up if they feel they're being treated unfairly. You don't want to be known as the company that mistreats its employees or doesn't pay them fairly.

In addition to the legal and reputational risks, fines and penalties for non-compliance can be a significant burden for a new business. It's better to be proactive and avoid getting caught off guard. Thankfully, there are several self-serve programs available, such as Gusto and Quickbooks, that can help you navigate the complexities of payroll and HR while freeing up your time and energy to focus on growing your business.

These self-serve programs can streamline your payroll process by handling tasks like calculating employee taxes and generating pay stubs. They also provide tools for managing employee benefits, such as health insurance and retirement plans. In addition, they can assist with compliance by automatically keeping track of federal and state labor laws.

While self-serve programs can be a cost-effective solution for managing payroll and HR, it's important to note that they do require some level of knowledge and experience to use effectively. You'll need to have a basic understanding of tax regulations, labor laws, and other compliance issues to ensure that you're following all the necessary guidelines. However, with some research and education, these programs can be a great option for small business owners who are looking to save time and money by managing payroll and HR in-house. So don't be afraid to embrace technology and take advantage of these tools to help your business succeed!

When it comes to HR, you gotta have your ducks in a row. That means establishing clear policies and procedures right from the get-go. And what's the best way to do that? Create an employee hand-book! It's like a guidebook for your team, outlining your company's policies, their rights, and their responsibilities. Plus, it can protect your business in case of any legal disputes or compliance issues. Can I get an "amen"?

Your employee handbook should cover a lot of ground. We're talking company policies and procedures, employment classifica-tions, benefits, time off, performance expectations, and code of conduct. You want to make sure it's up-to-date with current labor laws and regulations to avoid any legal mishaps.

But wait! You can't just hand out your employee handbook and think your job is done. It's not a "do as I say, not as I do" situation. You need to lead by example! If you have a dress code policy in your hand-book, you better show up looking sharp. And if you tell your employees not to smoke on the premises, you better not be sneaking a quick puff behind the building.

Following your own rules isn't just about setting a good example - it also shows that you respect your own policies and that you're committed to creating a positive work environment. It helps to build trust and credibility with your employees, and it ensures that everyone is held to the same standards.

So don't forget to take a good look at your employee handbook and make sure you're following all the rules too. You don't want to be known as the boss who talks the talk but can't walk the walk.

By providing your employees with an employee handbook, you can set expectations and create a positive work culture. It's like a North Star that guides your team to success. It can also help prevent misunderstandings or conflicts, which is great because nobody likes drama at work. And it promotes consistency in the way your business operates.

Chapter 33

AGREEMENTS

Agreements are an integral part of our lives, whether we realize it or not. They can take many forms, such as a handshake, a contract, or a simple understanding. At their core, agreements are a way to establish mutual expectations, boundaries, and responsibilities between individuals or groups.

In a social context, agreements can take the form of social norms or unwritten rules that govern our behavior and interactions with others. For example, we may agree to respect each other's personal space or to adhere to a set of social customs or traditions.

Even in a personal context, we make agreements with ourselves, whether it's to exercise regularly, eat healthier, or practice self-care. By setting clear expectations and holding ourselves accountable, we can improve our well-being and achieve our personal goals.

In a professional context, agreements are often established through employment contracts, service agreements, warranties and other legal documents. These agreements outline the terms and conditions of a working relationship, including job responsibilities, compensation, and benefits.

When an employee enters into an employment agreement with a business, they are agreeing to exchange their time and expertise for compensation. In essence, the business is purchasing the time and skills of the employee as part of this agreement.

Regardless of the context, agreements are a part of our lives, and by honoring them, we can build trust, strengthen relationships, and create a more harmonious and fulfilling life. When we fail to honor our agreements, we risk damaging our relationships and eroding the trust that is the foundation to any healthy and productive interaction.

At its core, business is a series of agreements between parties. Customers provide money in exchange for a product or service that a business offers, and it's crucial to establish clear terms and conditions to ensure a successful transaction.

Contracts and warranties can help to establish mutual expectations and responsibilities, and can provide legal protection for both the business and the customer. Clear communication is also pivotal in any business transaction, whether it's in person or online, to ensure that both parties understand the terms of the agreement.

But beyond the legalities of doing business, it's important to establish a culture of honesty, trust, and respect. By treating customers with fairness and transparency, businesses can build long-term relationships and establish a reputation for reliability and professionalism.

Doing business is about more than just making agreements and transactions. By focusing on ethical and sustainable practices, businesses can contribute to the greater good and make a meaningful difference in the lives of their customers and communities. While clear terms and conditions, warranties, and contracts are important to ensure a smooth and successful transaction, it's also important to establish a culture of honesty, trust, and respect.

Agreements can be challenging, and not every agreement comes easily. Sometimes, despite the best intentions, things just don't work out. This is true in all areas of life, including business and personal relationships.

While it's important to prioritize customer satisfaction and make every effort to meet their needs, it's also important to recognize that not every customer is the right fit for every business. Just like in personal relationships, sometimes a business and a customer are simply not a good match. And that's okay!

At the end of the day, it's about finding a balance between providing exceptional service and protecting the interests of your business. By being honest and transparent with customers and recognizing when it's time to move on, businesses can focus on building relationships with the right customers.

Don't over promise or make commitments that you can't keep. Instead, focus on creating clear, concise contracts that outline exactly what services you offer and what is considered "extra" or outside the scope of the agreement.

Communication is key! Make sure your customers understand what they can expect from your business, and be open to feedback and suggestions for improvement. By being transparent and upfront, you can avoid misunderstandings and build stronger relationships with your customers, even if they ultimately decide to take their business elsewhere.

COMMON SERVICE CONTRACT TERMS

1. **Information of Both Parties:** The contract should begin by clearly identifying the parties involved, including your business's full legal name and any alternative names, as well as the customer's legal name as it appears on official documentation. Avoid using nicknames, usernames, or stage names.

2. **Terms and Scope of the Project:** For service contracts, it's crucial to provide a detailed, precise, and clear description of the purpose and scope of the work, without using overly technical terms or legal jargon. This will help ensure that both parties agree on what the customer is paying for and what you will provide.

3. **Description of Goods or Services:** For goods or services provided in exchange for payment, a detailed itemization should be provided to clarify what is being sold and to establish professional limitations. Be sure to describe each item or service clearly, and state whether goods are being sold "as is."

4. **Payment Terms:** Clearly explaining how the buyer will purchase your goods or services is crucial for establishing a binding contract. You can outline payment terms such as a one-time payment, installments, or a subscription model, and list approved payment methods, such as bank checks, credit cards, and wire transfers.

5. **Schedule and Deadlines for Work:** Defining a schedule and deadline for service contracts will prevent disputes and ensure that the task is completed to the customer's satisfaction. Negotiate these with your customers and make sure you have adequate time to perform the task to avoid producing subpar results.

6. **Termination Clause:** Including a termination clause in your contract gives both parties the right to end the agreement at any time, where you can set requirements and penalties for cancellations or breaches of contract. For example, you may require a 30-day notice for service termination or specify an early termination fee.

7. **Signature of Both Parties:** To establish the binding nature of the document, close your customer agreement with signatures from both parties, including the signature date and the effective date. This ensures that you and the customer agree on the nature of the document as it is on the day it is signed, and can prevent future misunderstandings.

Physical Products

If your business deals with physical products, it's important to have a clear and fair warranty policy in place. A warranty can provide peace of mind to your customers and help establish trust in your brand.

When creating your warranty policy, make sure it's something you can realistically honor. Don't promise the world if you can't deliver. Be clear about what is covered and what isn't, and make sure the terms are easy for your customers to understand.

Consider the length of your warranty. Is it fair for the type of product you're selling? Is it comparable to warranties offered by your competitors? These are all important questions to ask when creating your policy.

Remember, a warranty is not just a legal document, it's also a marketing tool. By offering a fair and transparent warranty, you can show your customers that you stand behind your products and care about their satisfaction. So, take the time to create a warranty policy that is both practical and customer-friendly, and you'll be on your way to building a loyal and satisfied customer base.

COMMON WARRANTY TERMS

1. **Duration:** The length of time that the warranty is valid, which can range from a few months to several years.
2. **Coverage:** The specific components or features of the product that are covered by the warranty, as well as any exclusions or limitations.
3. **Remedies:** The options available to the customer if the product fails to meet the warranty terms, such as repair, replacement, or refund.
4. **Conditions:** The requirements or obligations that the customer must meet to be eligible for the warranty, such as proper use, maintenance, and storage of the product.
5. **Transferability:** Whether the warranty can be transferred to a new owner if the product is sold or gifted.
6. **Disclaimers:** Any statements that limit the liability of the manufacturer or seller, such as disclaimers for incidental or consequential damages.

It is important for both the manufacturer or seller and the customer to clearly understand the terms of a warranty to avoid any confusion or disputes in the future.

In addition to contracts and warranties, there are other important rules that businesses must follow. One such important rule is the set of terms and conditions listed on your website. These terms encompass a range of topics, including customer data management, intellectual property, refund policies, contact information, and other business policies.

To provide top-notch customer service, it's crucial to have clear and open communication with your customers. Being upfront about the terms, conditions, warranties, and contracts related to your products or services helps prevent any misunderstandings or potential legal issues. Keep in mind that not every customer will be a perfect fit for your business, and it's important to handle such situations with diplomacy, tact, and fairness to ensure that neither party feels wronged.

So, take the time to carefully craft your terms and conditions and make sure they're readily available to your customers. With clear communication, you can build strong relationships with your customers and establish a positive reputation for your business.

Chapter 34

TAX DEDUCTIONS

While taxes can be daunting, taking advantage of tax deductions can save you a boatload of money. But where to begin? Here are some tips to help you sail smoothly through tax deductions.

First, it's important to understand what tax deductions are. Tax deductions are expenses that you can subtract from your taxable income, thereby reducing the amount of tax you owe. Some common tax deductions for small businesses include office expenses, travel expenses, and marketing and advertising expenses.

Now, let's look at some ways you can maximize your tax deductions and keep more money in your pocket.

COMMON BUSINESS TAX DEDUCTIONS

1. **Home Office Deduction** - If you work from home, you may be able to claim a deduction for your home office expenses. This deduction allows you to deduct a portion of your mortgage interest, property taxes, utilities, and other home-related expenses.

2. **Business Travel Expenses** - If you travel for business purposes, you may be able to deduct your transportation costs, lodging, meals, and other related expenses.

3. **Advertising and Marketing Expenses** - Advertising and marketing expenses, such as business cards, flyers, and online ads, are generally deductible as a business expense.

4. **Vehicle Expenses** - If you use a vehicle for business purposes, you may be able to deduct expenses such as miles, gas, maintenance, and repairs.

5. **Supplies and Materials** - Expenses for supplies and materials used in your business, such as office supplies, inventory, and raw materials, are typically deductible.

6. **Insurance Premiums** - Premiums for various types of insurance, such as liability, property, and workers' compensation insurance, are generally deductible.

7. **Payroll** - The money a business pays to its employees, including salaries, wages, bonuses, and benefits

8. **Charitable Contributions** - Donations to charitable organizations are generally deductible, subject to certain limits.

MAXIMIZING YOUR TAX DEDUCTIONS

1. **Keep Accurate Records** - Your bookkeeping software comes into play here. Keeping accurate records of your business expenses is a must for maximizing your tax deductions. Make sure to save receipts and other documentation for all of your business-related expenses.

2. **Be Aware of Limitations** - Some tax deductions have limitations or restrictions that you need to be aware of. For example, the home office deduction is only available if you use a portion of your home exclusively for business purposes.

3. **Work with a Tax Professional** - Working with a qualified tax professional can help ensure that you are taking advantage of all available tax deductions and avoiding any potential issues with the IRS.

4. **Don't Overlook Small Expenses** - Even small expenses can add up over time and may be eligible for tax deductions. Make sure to keep track of all of your business-related expenses, no matter how small.

5. **Understand the Tax Code** - The tax code is complex and constantly changing. Take the time to educate yourself about the various tax deductions that are available to your business.

Honestly, nobody likes giving their money to Uncle Sam, and tax deductions are like finding money in the pocket of a jacket you haven't worn in ages - it feels pretty darn good! On to the next chapter.

Chapter 35

METRICS AND ANALYTICS

Alright, let's talk metrics and analytics. I know, I know, it sounds about as exciting as watching paint dry or grass grow, but bear with me here. As a business owner, you need to keep track of things like sales numbers, website traffic, customer demographics, and other metrics that will help you make informed decisions about your business. It's like having a secret decoder ring that tells you what's working and what's not. Plus, if you're anything like me, there's just something satisfying about looking at a bunch of charts and graphs and pretending you're a mad scientist plotting world domination. So go ahead, embrace your inner nerd, and start tracking those metrics like a boss!

COMMON METRICS AND REPORTS

- **Revenue:** is the cold hard cash your business is bringing in. Keep track of it to see how sales are performing and spot areas where you can improve.
- **Expenses:** are the opposite of revenue. This is where all your hard-earned dough goes, from salaries to rent to that fancy espresso machine you just had to have. Keeping track of expenses can help you spot areas where you can cut costs and save some cash.

- **Profit margin:** is the sweet spot between revenue and expenses. It's the money you have left after everything else is paid for. Keep an eye on your profit margin to make sure your business is sustainable and profitable.
- **Conversion rate:** is the percentage of website visitors who do what you want them to do, like buy your stuff or sign up for your newsletter. Improving your conversion rate can help you increase sales and grow your business.
- **Customer acquisition cost:** is the amount of money it costs to get a new customer. Keep track of this metric to figure out the most effective marketing and advertising channels for your biz.
- **Customer retention rate:** is the percentage of customers who stick around and keep doing business with you. Make sure you're providing top-notch customer service and value to keep them coming back for more.
- **Supply Cost:** is the cost of the goods or services you sell. Keep track of this so you can price your offerings properly and ensure you're making a profit.
- **Website traffic:** is the number of people visiting your website. Keeping track of website traffic can help you spot areas where you can improve your site to attract more visitors and keep them engaged.
- **Social media engagement:** is the level of love your social media posts are getting, from likes to comments to shares. Use this data to help you create the most effective content and messaging to connect with your audience.

Every business is different, so the key metrics you need to focus on may vary. The important thing is to pay attention to the numbers that matter most to your business. It's easy to get caught up in the day-to-day operations of your business and forget to monitor your key performance indicators (KPIs). Take the time to identify the metrics that are most relevant to your business. You'll have a better understanding of your business's performance and be better equipped to make informed decisions to drive growth and success.

Chapter 36

FRIENDS WITH BENEFITS

If you are wondering what this book on business has to do with your friends, the answer is a lot. Your inner circle plays a crucial role in your personal and professional growth.

The law of averages, the theory that the result of any given situation will be the average of all outcomes, also applies to the people you spend the most time with.

Take a moment and close your eyes. Imagine the people in your life - your mentors, family, and friends. Now, think about the impact they have on you. Are they a positive or negative influence? Do they challenge you to grow and achieve your goals, or do they hold you back?

Try this influence rating exercise: Write down the names of five people you spend the most time with and assign a numerical value to each person from 1 to 10, based on the positive influence they have on your life (with 10 being the most positive influence possible). Then, calculate your average. This can help you see how each person affects your average and give you insight into how they contribute to your success or hold you back.

1. _____   4. _____

2. _____   5. _____

3. _____   **Combined Average:** _____

You want to surround yourself with people who are more accomplished than you in different areas and can offer you different perspectives. When assessing the people in your inner circle, consider how they impact your mindset, motivation, and actions. Do they encourage you to take risks and step outside of your comfort zone? Do they offer constructive criticism and feedback that helps you grow? Do they inspire you to be a better person and entrepreneur?

Your friends and the people you surround yourself with can have a significant impact on many aspects of your life. For example, in a recent study from the Framingham Heart Study, which is one of the largest and longest-running health studies ever conducted, it was found that if a friend of yours becomes obese, you are 45 percent more likely to gain weight over the next two years.

This study shows just how influential the people in our lives can be. Audit the people around you and make sure that you're spending time with people who are in line with what you want for your own life. Surrounding yourself with people who have healthy habits, positive attitudes, and similar goals can inspire you to adopt those same habits and attitudes and help you achieve your goals.

If you find that some of the people in your inner circle are holding you back or bringing negative energy into your life, it may be time to reassess or minimize those relationships. It's not always easy to let go of people, but it's necessary for your personal and professional growth. Surrounding yourself with the right people is not a guarantee of success, but it can make a significant difference in your journey.

You've likely heard stories of people who lost everything, yet managed to rebuild their wealth from scratch. These success stories often boil down to one crucial factor: the people they surround themselves with. I don't mean to sound overconfident, but if I were to lose everything I have today - my house, my money, my business - I'm confident that I could rebuild it within a few years. Why? Because I have two powerful resources at my disposal: knowledge and a strong network.

Firstly, I have the knowledge and skills required to rebuild my life. I've learned how to be resilient, resourceful, and strategic in my approach to business. I know how to identify opportunities and take calculated risks. But even with all this knowledge, I wouldn't be able to do it alone.

That's where the second factor comes in: my network of successful entrepreneurs. These are not my high school buddies; they're individuals I've met through various mentorship programs, business events, and networking opportunities. These are people who have already achieved what I aspire to accomplish, and they're willing to share their knowledge and expertise to help me succeed.

Having a strong network of successful people is critical to achieving success. They can provide guidance, support, and connections to help you overcome obstacles and achieve your goals. And in times of crisis, they can be a lifeline, offering valuable resources and advice to help you get back on your feet.

Success isn't just about what you know; it's also about who you know. Creating a robust network of accomplished individuals can help you reach your objectives and overcome setbacks. So, take the time to attend networking events, join mentorship programs, and connect with other entrepreneurs. Surround yourself with people who can help you succeed, and you'll be well on your way to achieving your dreams.

Chapter 37

WORK-LIFE HABITS

Welcome to the chapter on habits! Habits are the building blocks of success. Every successful business person knows that developing good habits is key to achieving their goals. And as an entrepreneur, developing healthy habits is crucial to keeping you going in the long run.

Why? Because bad habits can jeopardize your health, waste your time, and drain your energy.

HEALTH: Entrepreneurship requires a lot of dedication, hard work, and perseverance. It can be a long and challenging journey, and to succeed, you need to be at the top of your health game. You need to have the energy, stamina, and mental clarity to make important decisions, tackle challenges, and stay focused on your goals.

Without good health, you won't be able to achieve your dreams or do anything that you set out to do. But with good habits, a healthy body and mind, you can run the marathon you're about to get into. Taking care of your health should be your top priority.

Think about it - what happens when you get sick or unwell? Your business may suffer, and your employees may struggle to keep things going. If you're a one-person show, your business will come to a halt. This is why you should develop better health habits that will help you avoid these setbacks and keep your business running smoothly.

Better health habits can mean different things to different people. For you, it could mean exercising, drinking more water, giving up drinking, or practicing stress-relieving techniques like meditation or yoga. Whatever they are, make it a priority to exercise regularly, eat well, and get enough rest. These habits will give you the strength and energy you need to tackle any challenge that comes your way.

In addition to physical health, it's also crucial to take care of your mental health. Entrepreneurship can be stressful, and it's easy to get overwhelmed with the demands of running a business.

MAINTAIN GOOD MENTAL HEALTH

1. **Practice mindfulness:** Mindfulness is a technique that involves being present in the moment and observing your thoughts and feelings without judgment. It can help reduce stress and anxiety, improve focus and concentration, and increase self-awareness. Make a habit of incorporating mindfulness into your daily routine by practicing meditation, yoga, or deep breathing exercises.

2. **Seek support:** Running a business can be isolating, and it's easy to feel like you're carrying the weight of the world on your shoulders. Seek out support from friends, family, or colleagues who understand the challenges of entrepreneurship. Consider joining a peer support group or finding a mentor who can offer guidance and advice.

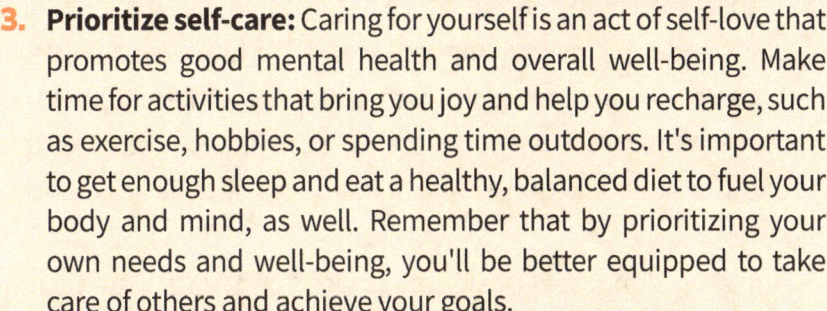

3. **Prioritize self-care:** Caring for yourself is an act of self-love that promotes good mental health and overall well-being. Make time for activities that bring you joy and help you recharge, such as exercise, hobbies, or spending time outdoors. It's important to get enough sleep and eat a healthy, balanced diet to fuel your body and mind, as well. Remember that by prioritizing your own needs and well-being, you'll be better equipped to take care of others and achieve your goals.

4. **Learn to manage stress:** Stress is a natural part of entrepreneurship, but it's important to learn healthy ways to manage it. Practice relaxation techniques, such as deep breathing or visualization, and prioritize self-care to reduce stress levels. Consider outsourcing tasks that are causing excessive stress, or delegating responsibilities to employees or contractors.

5. **Consider therapy or counseling:** If you're struggling with mental health issues, consider seeking out therapy or counseling. A mental health professional can help you work through challenges, develop coping strategies, and improve your overall well being.

Ultimately, your health is your most valuable asset as an entrepreneur. By taking care of yourself, you're investing in the success of your business and your own personal growth. So, make it a priority to prioritize your health and wellbeing!

VISION: Entrepreneurs who achieve great success, have a clear vision of what they want to achieve. They don't allow themselves to get bogged down in the day-to-day details of running a business. Instead, they focus on the big picture and consistently create clear visions for themselves. History is rife with examples of visionary leaders who have transformed the world through their visions.

Martin Luther King Jr.'s famous "I Have a Dream" speech articulated a clear vision of a society that judged people by their character rather than the color of their skin. This vision inspired a generation and catalyzed significant changes in civil rights laws and policies.

Steve Jobs' vision for Apple was to create revolutionary products that would change the way people live and work. His relentless pursuit of this vision made Apple one of the most valuable companies in the world.

Similarly, Elon Musk's vision for SpaceX and Tesla is to push the boundaries of innovation and create a more sustainable future. His dedication to this vision has inspired a new generation and led to groundbreaking advancements in the fields of space travel and electric vehicles.

These leaders illustrate the power of having a clear and compelling vision. While you may not aim to change the world, having a vision of what you want to achieve is essential to success. It gives you direction, purpose, and motivation to pursue your goals with passion and conviction. Whether you are starting a new business or pursuing a personal endeavor, a clear vision can be the driving force behind your success.

Before you begin visualizing your future, define what success means to you personally. Success is not solely about financial gain; it can be about living a fulfilling life, making a positive impact in the world, retiring early, or leaving a legacy for your children. Take time to reflect on what truly matters to you in life and ensure that your vision aligns with your business goals. This alignment will help you stay motivated and focused, making it more likely that you will achieve both personal and professional success.

Once you've defined success for yourself, you can start visualizing your ideal life. Think about different aspects of your life, such as your business, relationships, health, and personal growth. Imagine what your life would look like if you achieved your goals in each area.

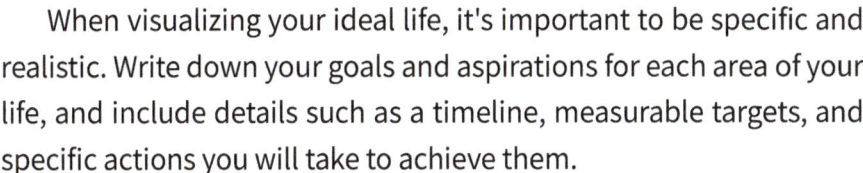

When visualizing your ideal life, it's important to be specific and realistic. Write down your goals and aspirations for each area of your life, and include details such as a timeline, measurable targets, and specific actions you will take to achieve them.

Remember that achieving your vision takes consistent effort, and it's okay to make adjustments as you go. Review your vision regularly and celebrate your progress along the way. With a clear vision and a commitment to taking action, you can achieve the life and success you truly desire.

Try this visualization exercise: Take a moment to close your eyes, take a deep breath, and let your mind wander to the future - five years from now. Envision yourself at the pinnacle of success with your business, living the life you've always dreamed of. What do you see? What does your day-to-day look like? What have you accomplished that fills you with pride?

Now, take a pen and paper and jot down your vision. Keep it somewhere safe, where you can easily access it. Let this vision be your beacon of light as you navigate the journey of entrepreneurship. Allow it to guide you and keep you focused, even when the road ahead feels long and uncertain. And remember, with hard work and determination, that future is within your reach.

GOALS: Setting too many goals will absolutely lead to burnout and misery, especially if they don't align with your vision and health habits. Instead, take a step back and create goals that give you clarity around your future and what you want to achieve. This can help you focus on what truly matters and avoid getting sidetracked by goals that don't align with your overall vision.

Having a clear life vision and aligned goals will help you to achieve success and create a fulfilling life. It gives you a sense of purpose and direction, and helps you stay motivated even when things get tough. So take the time to align your goals with your vision and health habits.

Make sure your goals are SMART - specific, measurable, achievable, relevant, and time-bound. This means setting goals that are clear and well-defined, with specific metrics that you can use to track your progress. Your goals should also be achievable and relevant to your big-picture vision, with a realistic timeline for completion.

To ensure that you stay on track, make a plan for achieving each goal, with specific action steps and deadlines. Review your progress regularly and make adjustments as needed. Celebrate your successes along the way, and use setbacks as learning opportunities to improve your approach.

Make it a habit to do at least one thing every day that brings you closer to your goal. It doesn't have to be a huge task - even small steps can add up over time.In addition to daily goals, create weekly and yearly goals that build upon each other to move you closer to your vision. This way, you'll have a roadmap for where you're headed, and you'll be able to stay motivated and on track.Remember that it's okay to adjust your goals as needed along the way. Life is unpredictable, and sometimes unexpected challenges or opportunities may arise that require you to change your course. Stay flexible and adaptable, and don't be afraid to pivot if necessary.

ORGANIZATION: Life is full of unexpected challenges and distractions that can easily derail your plans. That's why it's imperative to be organized and focused, so you can channel your energy into what truly matters. Don't let excuses or the chaos of the day control your destiny. You have the power to take control of your life and make things happen. But to get there, you need to organize yourself, your time, and your surroundings. By doing so, you'll be able to plan your day, crush your goals like a productivity ninja, and achieve your entrepreneurial and personal dreams.

It's easy to get stuck in a reactive mode, where you're constantly putting out fires and waiting for the next emergency to come up. But this mindset won't get you anywhere. To grow and thrive, you need to adopt a growth mindset and be proactive. Take charge of your life by setting goals, making plans, and taking action. If you want to take a vacation, book a ticket! Don't wait around for it to magically happen. By making organization a habit, you can focus your energy on what you can control and create the life you want.

Organizing is not just a nice-to-have, it's a must-have. It's one of the key ingredients for success, promoting increased productivity, reduced stress, better time management, and improved decision-making. By adopting an organized mindset and developing good habits, you can achieve greater success and happiness in all aspects of your life. So, don't wait another day. Take action now and start organizing!

ORGANIZATION TIPS

1. **Create a plan:** Start by creating a plan for your day, week, or month. This can help you prioritize your tasks and stay on track. Make sure to include both short-term and long-term goals, and break them down into manageable steps.
2. **Use a to-do list:** Write down everything you need to do, and cross off each task as you complete it. This gives you something to measure each week and helps you hold yourself accountable.

3. **Declutter:** Get rid of anything that you don't need or use regularly. This can help you create a more organized and functional space, both physically and digitally. Declutter your inbox, remove apps from your phone that you don't use, and tidy up your workspace. If you feel overwhelmed or unsure where to start, consider hiring a professional organizer who can provide help!

4. **Develop a routine:** Establish a daily routine that works for you. This can help you stay on track and ensure that you're using your time effectively. Make sure to include time for exercise, relaxation, and self-care.

5. **Stay flexible:** Remember that life can be unpredictable, and you may need to adjust your plans or routines from time to time. Stay flexible and be willing to adapt as needed. Don't be too hard on yourself if things don't go as planned. Learn to embrace change and find ways to make it work for you.

Create a system that aligns with your unique needs and preferences. Take some time to reflect on when you feel most energized, inspired, and productive, and use that insight to design your schedule. Don't feel pressured to conform to a schedule that doesn't fit your natural rhythms and preferences. If you're not a morning person, don't sweat it! Instead, use that time for activities that bring you joy or require less mental effort, so you can ease into your day in a way that feels natural and comfortable for you.

Keep in mind that everyone has their own way of doing things, and what works for you might not work for your colleagues, partners, or employees. There is no one size fits all solution. With the pandemic, people have had the chance to work from home and better understand their individual personalities, work styles, and priorities. Work to be open-minded and flexible when it comes to creating

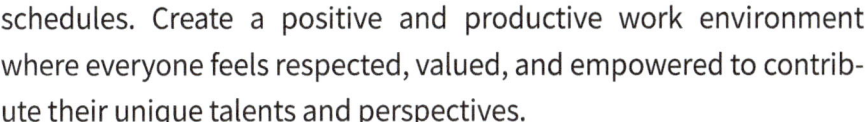

schedules. Create a positive and productive work environment where everyone feels respected, valued, and empowered to contribute their unique talents and perspectives.

Effective organization is all about finding a system that feels empowering and natural for you, while also respecting the individual needs and preferences of those around you. By doing so, you can unleash your full potential, build strong relationships, and create a work environment that fosters growth, innovation, and success. Don't be afraid to take ownership of your schedule and create a system that works for you – the possibilities are endless!.

BALANCE: Owning a business doesn't mean it has to be all work and no play! When you decided to start your own business, you likely did so because you wanted the freedom to choose how you spend your time. Remember that feeling, and make sure to prioritize it! As a new entrepreneur, you might feel like there aren't enough hours in the day. And the truth is there isn't. You need to make the ones you have count.

Balancing work and personal life can be a tricky act to master, especially for entrepreneurs in the early stages of building their business. But letting work consume your life is like running a marathon without taking any water breaks - you might make it to the finish line, but you'll be severely dehydrated and exhausted! It's important to make time for the things you love outside of work, whether it's spending time with family, pursuing a hobby, or simply taking a few moments to relax. Your personal and professional lives are interconnected, and taking care of one can contribute to the success of the other.

Don't fall into the trap of thinking that you have to do everything alone or that your business should consume all of your time and energy. Maintaining a healthy work-life balance is crucial for your personal and professional success.

Remember, it's not lonely at the top if you prioritize your relationships and invest in yourself. If you don't make prioritizing yourself a habit, you'll end up feeling burnt out and unhappy. Take care of yourself and make time for the things you enjoy outside of work. Don't feel guilty about taking a break or scheduling time for yourself. Your personal and professional lives are interconnected, and taking care of one can contribute to the success of the other.

Spicy Tip: When you're feeling stuck, change your state! Changing your state is a game-changer for regaining momentum and inspiration. The best way to do this is by physically moving your body or location. Stand up, take a break, and stretch your body to release tension and increase blood flow. Another option is to change up your workspace. Rearrange your setup or move your desk to a new location. This change of scenery can provide a fresh perspective and stimulate new ideas and ways of thinking. So, next time you're feeling stuck, try incorporating some movement to help spark your creativity and get back on track.

CELEBRATE: It's easy to get caught up in the daily grind and lose sight of our accomplishments. We often have our sights set on the next big goal or project, without taking a moment to appreciate the progress we've made. However, making it a habit to celebrate your wins - no matter how small they may seem - can drastically improve your personal and professional growth.

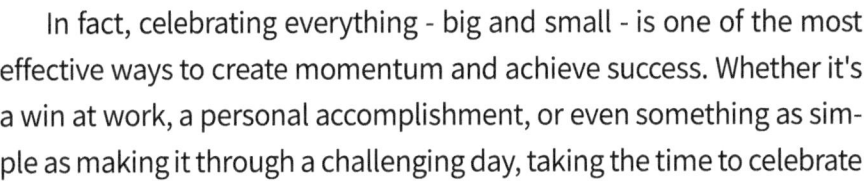

In fact, celebrating everything - big and small - is one of the most effective ways to create momentum and achieve success. Whether it's a win at work, a personal accomplishment, or even something as simple as making it through a challenging day, taking the time to celebrate can have a profound impact on our lives.

Celebrating your wins can help you find joy and stay motivated. It's not just about you, either. Celebrating your accomplishments also fosters a positive and supportive workplace culture. When you take the time to acknowledge and appreciate your progress, it inspires others to do the same.

Even the smallest of achievements should be celebrated. Whether you landed a new client, purchased a new company truck, or hit your first $10,000, take the time to acknowledge and appreciate it. Celebrating these wins can be as simple as treating yourself and your team to lunch or a small party, or sharing the good news on social media.

As a leader, it's your role to be a cheerleader for your team, celebrating their accomplishments and milestones. When you acknowledge and appreciate their hard work, you inspire them to continue pushing forward and achieving more. And it's not just about work - celebrate your friends and loved ones, too. A little recognition and encouragement can go a long way in creating positive relationships and building stronger connections.

Humans are wired to respond to rewards, and celebrating successes provides that sweet reward that our brains crave. By creating a culture of celebration, you'll create momentum that propels you and your team forward towards even greater achievements.

As this book comes to a close, take a moment to celebrate your accomplishment of finishing it! Whether it's treating yourself to a nice dinner, spending time with loved ones, or simply taking a moment to reflect on what you've learned, find a way to reward yourself for a job well done. Remember, it's important to recognize and celebrate your accomplishments, no matter how small, to foster your personal and professional growth. So, don't forget to acknowledge and appreciate your wins, and create a culture of celebration that inspires others to do the same.

Chapter 38

THE LAST CHAPTER

Hey there, friend! It looks like you've reached the end of this book, and it's time to say goodbye. But don't worry, the end of this book is just the beginning of your journey.

Starting a business is not for the faint of heart, but if you have a passion for what you do and the drive to see it through, there's no limit to what you can achieve. Remember to stay positive, even when things don't go as planned. Fear and doubt may try to hold you back, but they're just illusions. It's important to remember that fear is often rooted in false evidence that seems real to us, leading us to avoid situations or take risks. By challenging your fears and seeking out accurate information, you can overcome them. Don't let fear stop you from achieving your goals!

And when you do stumble, don't give up. Failure is not the end, but an opportunity to learn and grow. Take the lessons you've learned and use them to move forward.

Embrace change and be open to new ideas. The only constant in life is change, and in the world of business, it's even more true. Be willing to adapt and pivot, and don't be afraid to take calculated risks. You never know where they might lead you.

So go out there and create your dreams! The road may be long and difficult, but the journey is well worth it. And if you ever need a reminder, just flip through the pages of this book and remember all the lessons you've learned.

Until next time, stay passionate, stay driven, and keep pushing forward. The sky's the limit!

Sincerely,

Natalia Alaine

P. S Throughout this book, we've talked about the importance of hard work, perseverance, and celebrating wins. But there's one more ingredient that's critical to achieving success, and that's you. That's right, you are the secret sauce! You have everything it takes to accomplish your goals and reach your full potential.

Just the fact that you've made it this far shows that you're committed and have what it takes to succeed. You are amazing and have unique talents and abilities that set you apart from everyone else. It's time to unleash your full potential and go after what you want in life.

Remember, success is not just about making money or achieving fame. It's about finding joy, being a good boss, having a company that makes a difference, and creating a fulfilling life. You have the power to make a positive impact in the world, and it all starts with believing in yourself and your abilities.

I can't wait to see the successes that come your way as you continue to work hard and pursue your dreams. So, keep pushing forward, and never forget that you are the secret sauce that makes everything possible.

If you found value in this book, I would be incredibly grateful if you could take a moment to leave a review. Your feedback helps me to improve and continue providing valuable content for aspiring business owners like you.

Also, be sure to check out my website at BusinessOwners-SecretSauce.com. You'll find helpful links, resources, and a contact form where you can share any feedback, ideas, or questions you may have. I'm always happy to connect with like-minded entrepreneurs and help in any way I can.

Scan here to visit the website:

www.ingramcontent.com/pod-product-compliance
Lightning Source LLC
Chambersburg PA
CBHW070705130626

46553CB00005B/1847